Santa Fe
A Pictorial History

Donning Company/Publishers
Norfolk/Virginia Beach

design by Philip Johnson

Santa Fe
A Pictorial History

by John Sherman

The Donning Company/Publishers
5659 Virginia Beach Boulevard
Norfolk, Virginia 23502

**Library of Congress Cataloging in Publication
Data:**

Santa Fe, a pictorial history

　Bibliography: p.
　Includes index.
　1. Santa Fe, N.M.—Description—Views.
2. Santa Fe, N.M.—History—Pictorial works.
I. Sherman, John.
F804.S243S26　　　978.9'56　　　80-39666
ISBN 0-89865-350-9 (hbk.)
ISBN 0-89865-104-2 (pbk.)

This edition is being distributed exclusively by:

　William Gannon, Publisher
　143 Sombrio Drive
　Santa Fe, New Mexico 87501
　505-983-1579

Grateful acknowledgement is made to the First National Bank of Santa Fe and New Mexico Banquest Corporation for their introduction of the hardcover limited edition.

*To my wife Lois,
and to my children David and Chizoma,
my three favorite Santa Feans.*

Contents

Foreword

Illustrations of Santa Fe structures, street scenes and inhabitants appearing in books and articles about New Mexico and its capital have captured the interest of readers since army officers and other Anglo-American observers first published their reports and accounts following United States occupation in 1846. Throughout the succeeding years, and especially in this century, an increasing number of publications, in particular those directed towards enlightening visitors to the city, have made use of photographs. Historic structures meriting preservation have been well documented in the three editions of the Historic Santa Fe Foundation's *Old Santa Fe Today*. However, the examples selected for all these accounts have been relatively few in number and highly selective, and the same photograph has sometimes appeared in several different volumes.

In contrast, this book visually documents in comprehensive and systematic fashion the centuries-old history of the Santa Fe area, beginning even with the archeological evidence of those who lived here before the Spaniards arrived. Utilizing reproductions of plans, sketches, archival records, portraits, and particularly photographs, the author has narrated the story of the oldest capital from its founding in 1610 as a villa and the northernmost outpost of the Spanish colonial frontier through the development of its rich, multi-cultural heritage during three political sovereignties. Illustrations of buildings and street scenes throughout the decades since United States control, combined with bird's-eye view and recent aerial photographs graphically record the growth and changing character of the city. Paradoxically, however, much of the historic street pattern through the city and into the plaza area as it appeared in the 1766-68 Urrutia map of Santa Fe is still discernible in the aerial photographs, while the Palace of the Governors and various religious structures, or their successors, are still in the same locations.

The wealth of photographs, most of which have not previously been published, have been assembled from public and private depositories. Pictures of individual Santa Feans, past and present, garnered from family collections and albums, add an element of special human interest.

In common with many others who have researched, written about, painted, photographed or excavated in and around Santa Fe the author is a Santa Fean only by adoption. Migrating with his family from the outside world, he promptly came under the spell of the venerable villa and in this pictorial history he transmits some of its magical quality to his readers.

Myra Ellen Jenkins
Santa Fe, New Mexico

Preface

Santa Fe. There is a kind of magic about that name. It brings to the minds of many who have never even been there the vision of the nineteenth-century Santa Fe Trail; the Atchison, Topeka and Santa Fe trains; or the twentieth-century artists' colony. Or, perhaps, one remembers photos or paintings of the rounded corners of brown adobe walls against a cloudless, brilliant blue sky.

To those of us who live in Santa Fe, it is indeed all those things, but it is much more, too. It is a daily mixture of cultures—Spanish, Indian, Anglo—in a city that houses some of the country's oldest buildings, which often contain the most modern works of art or people with the most current of ideas.

This city is centuries-old Santa Fe Fiesta and decades-old Santa Fe Opera. It is Santa Fe Style—a way of architecture, interior design, and dress and, with all these, a way of life.

Centuries after the first settlements were made along what is now called the Santa Fe River, and eons after the first Indians traversed this area, visitors and Santa Feans see the same beautiful landscapes and skies that greeted those of former times.

Visitors to this city will often marvel aloud at the sheer beauty of the buildings outlined against the even more beautiful natural attractions—the mountains, sunsets, and skies. Though we see them every day, we who live here find those beauties just as fresh as any visitor does. They may well, in fact, be what drew us or our ancestors here. And they are what keep us.

For this book, I have gathered hundreds of photos, drawings, and maps of Santa Fe to illustrate the tremendous changes that have taken place not only since 1610, but since such dates as 1910 or 1960, as well. Santa Fe has survived those many changes and many conquerors over hundreds of years. It remains, essentially, Santa Fe.

Acknowledgments

Hundreds of people assisted in some way in the preparation of this book. I was gratified to have such splendid cooperation from so many individuals and organizations. Photos, names, and memories were shared with me freely in my pursuit of material to tell some of the wonderful story of Santa Fe. It is not possible to list all of those people here, but I do want to mention several who gave special assistance.

First, Dr. Myra Ellen Jenkins, who wrote the foreword, went over the drafts of this book with me and helped immensely in clarifying certain points of history. She made many valuable suggestions that I am very grateful for. I cannot express my thanks enough for the time and effort that went into her review of this book. She is truly a "historian's historian."

There were two major public collections of photographs that I used. Arthur Olivas and Richard Rudisill of the Museum of New Mexico's photo archives patiently handled my many questions and requests for photos over a period of many months. Mike Miller of the New Mexico State Records Center and Archives likewise gave me any assistance I asked for when I reviewed the center's files of photography and historic films.

Others that helped in the compiling of the material in this book include David Noble, School of American Research; Orlando Romero, New Mexico State Library; Barbaraellen Koch, the *Albuquerque Journal;* Stewart Peckham, Nancy Warren, and Nancy Fox, Laboratory of Anthropology; Hugo Hamilton, Santa Fe Opera; the Santa Fe Chamber Music Festival; Marcy Granada, Santa Fe Festival Theatre; Marcia Muth Miller and Sherry Smith-Gonzales, History Library of the Museum of New Mexico; Brother Abel, Christian Brothers; James Ball, St. Michael's High School; Elaine Horwitch Gallery; Mary Wormley, Museum of New Mexico; St. Catherine Indian School; Harry Moul, City Planning Office, City of Santa Fe; Bohannan and Houston; the Amon Carter Museum; Greg Van Pelt, Orchestra of Santa Fe; Christine Mather, International Folk Art Museum; Richard Levy, Silver Sunbeam; the staff of the Zimmerman Library, University of New Mexico; Kathleen Brooker, Historic Preservation Bureau; Larry Sanders, the *New Mexican;* Edwinna Bernat, New Mexico Banquest Corporation; Louann Jordan, Santa Fe Fiesta Council; Betty Ann Powell, Santa Fe Downs; Chicago City Ballet; Charlotte Roybal, St. Vincent's Hospital; Herman Agoyo, All-Indian Pueblo Council Tri-Centennial Commission; Doug Svetnicka, College of Santa Fe.

Also, T. B. Catron III; Fremont Ellis; Frances Dunne; Donald Van Soelen; John Candelario; Maria Benitez; Kay Wiest; Gladys Gilmour; John P. Conron; Reynalda Dinkel; Judith Brito; Julie Kaune; Consuelo Bergere Mendenhall; Amalia Sena Sanchez; Ollie McKenzie; Hansel Pflueger; Peter Van Dresser; Marjorie Gans; Concha Ortiz y Pino de Kleven; Mela Ortiz y Pino de Martin; Robert Martin; Anita Gonzales Thomas; Bert Prince; Anna Ortiz; Calla Hay; Harriet Kidder; Nancy Applegate; Paul Masters; Beatrice Chauvenet; Loring Sperry; Beaumont Newhall.

My wife Lois and my children David and Chizoma provided the kind of support any writer needs who has embarked on a project such as this. Not only did they give me the necessary quiet (and cups of coffee), but they simply made it possible for me to prepare this book.

Santa Fe

Chapter One
Before 1610:

The Anasazi

We tend to think of the beginning of Santa Fe in terms of the winter of 1609-10, when the Spanish soldiers and colonists began to construct the capital of New Mexico.

But, like most places established by Europeans and their descendants on the North American continent, the Native Americans had been there first.

Today, the existence of Native Americans in what is now Santa Fe is evident to many gardeners, construction workers, or others who examine the soil of the city. For, under the ground of much of Santa Fe can be found potsherds (pieces of prehistoric Native American pottery), weapons, and tools, discarded or abandoned by the area's original inhabitants.

According to Stewart Peckham, assistant director of the Museum of New Mexico's Laboratory of Anthropology, there were several pueblos (settlements) within the present city limits of Santa Fe prior to 1610.

Some of the sites were excavated earlier in this century by either the Laboratory of Anthropology or the School of American Research, both in Santa Fe. Artifacts found at the ancient pueblos were removed and are in storage or on display at those two institutions. In most cases, the sites were then covered back up, in hope that future archaeologists would have the chance to re-excavate and obtain further information about the ancient inhabitants.

One such site, named Arroyo Negro, on what is now West Alameda Street, was found to have tree rings that dated its founding to A.D. 1050-1150. Many others date from later centuries. Some, no doubt, have yet to be discovered. A few small settlements have already been destroyed by modern inhabitants ignorant of their existence or not interested in preserving remains of such old dwellings where the opportunity existed to build more modern ones.

The former inhabitants of these centuries-old pueblos are known as the Anasazi ("ancient ones") and are ancestors of today's Pueblo Indians who live on nineteen reservations in western and northern New Mexico.

Most of the Santa Fe-area pueblos were not established adjacent to the Santa Fe River or the area's creeks, but were placed on higher ground parallel to the water so that the land immediately next to the water could be used for irrigated farming. Placing the pueblo up high also afforded it protection from flooding and gave residents a better view of the immediate area, sometimes necessary for their safety.

The pueblos usually consisted of a series of small rooms. These were entered from the rooftops, with the aid of ladders which could be pulled down into the rooms in the event of an attack. Some of the residents of Taos Pueblo, north of Santa Fe, live today in five-story structures very similar to those found in the ancient pueblos of the Santa Fe area.

Religious life, and hence much of pueblo life, centered on the kiva, chambers often built underground, where each clan met separately to carry on the religious aspects of daily life.

Potsherds

These potsherds show a typical black-on-white pattern and were found at the Arroyo Negro Pueblo site. Arroyo Negro is believed to have been settled in the eleventh or twelfth centuries within what is now the Santa Fe limits.

Photo by John Sherman

Much of the culture, language, and customs of that era survive in the modern Pueblo Indian life. Visitors to the Santa Fe area may see dances not too unlike those performed centuries ago in such places as Arroyo Negro and the other pueblos in present-day Santa Fe.

When the Spanish arrived to build their capital, according to Peckham, the immediate area may have been uninhabited for at least 200 years. Drought was likely a factor in that abandonment of the many sites established along the Santa Fe River and its tributaries. After the Spanish established themselves in Santa Fe, Indians also came to live in the area once again, although many of them were not originally from this area but came with the Spanish from Mexico.

Pindi Plan

Pindi Pueblo, excavated in 1932-33 by the School of American Research, was found to have been established circa A.D. 1300. Pindi was on the north bank of the Santa Fe River, directly opposite the village of Agua Fria, about six miles from the then-city limits of Santa Fe on land owned by Jose Montoya, Ramon Montoya, Manuel Ortiz, and Joe Romero. This town plan is typical of those that existed in Santa Fe during the pre-Spanish era.

Map from Stubb and Stallings, Excavation of Pindi Pueblo

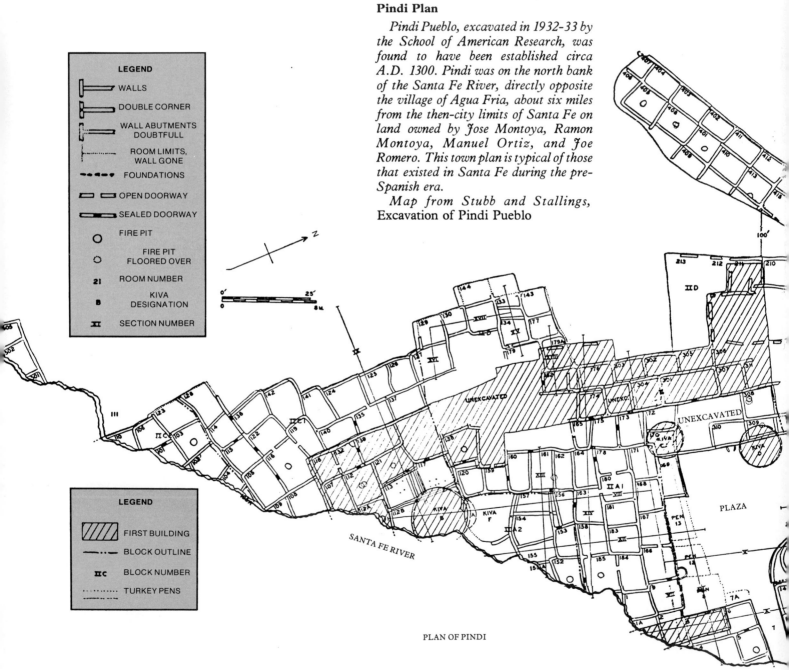

PLAN OF PINDI

Arroyo Hondo Excavation

Always cognizant of the people that preceded the Europeans to Santa Fe, the School of American Research continues to probe the origins of today's Pueblo Indians, among others. In the early 1970s, extensive excavation of the pueblo named Arroyo Hondo took place a few miles outside the city limits.

The scarcity of water, also a modern problem, made it necessary for the ancient peoples, the Anasazi, to abandon many of the area's pueblos; drought forced inhabitants to seek a livelihood elsewhere. This particular pueblo had been occupied for 125 years. Founded circa A.D. 1300, it was virtually abandoned circa 1350, reestablished, then finally abandoned circa 1425. This photo shows the small rooms of the pueblo.

Photo by David Noble; courtesy of the School of American Research

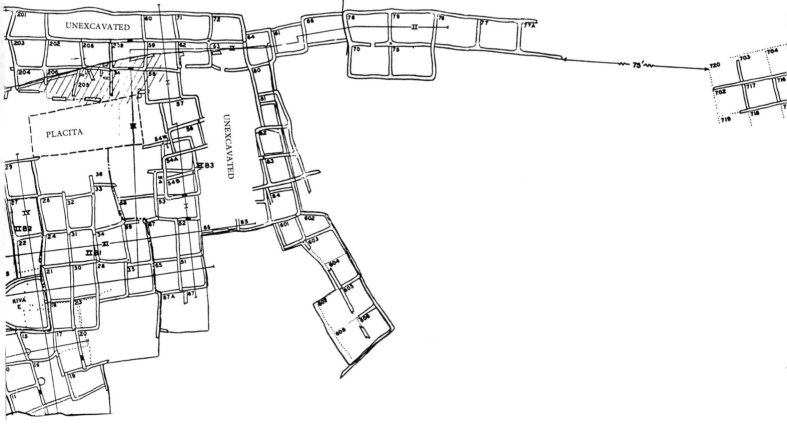

Don felipe por la gracia de Dios Rey de Castilla
de Leon, de las dos Sicilias, de Jerusalen, de Portugal,
de Navarra, de Granada, de Toledo, de Valencia, de
Galicia, de Mallorca, de Sevilla de Cerdeña de
Cordoba, de Corcega de Murcia, de Jaen de los Al-
garbes de Algecira, de Gibraltar, delas Islas de Can-
ria Yndias Islas y tierra firme del mar Oceano, Ar-
chiduque de Austria, Duque de Borgoña, bra-
bante y milan, Conde de Abspurg de flandes
y Tirol y Barzelona, Señor de Vizcaya y de
Molina &a. A Vos el venerable Padre fray esteban
de Perea dela orden de Seraphico san francisco
custodio delos Relixiosos dela dha orden que Resi-
den en las provincias de nueva Mexico, o a otro qualquiera
Relando cuyo cargo estubiere la dha custodia, Relixi-
oso de ella, Sabed, que en la Junta que el marques
de Guadalcazar pariente mi Virrey Gouern.or y Capp.an general
de las provincias de la nueva españa y presidente de
mi audiencia de Chancilleria Real que Reside en la
Ciudad de Mexico, hubo en Veinte y nueve de
Jullio deeste año con los tres oidores mas antiguos
dellos a mi audiencia presente mi fiscal en conformidad
de la orden que Tengo dado, se bieron algunas cartas
mias, memoriales Petiçiones y otros Recaudos que de
esas dhas provincias han despachado y escrito al dho
mi Virrey diferentes personas asi eclesiasticas como se-
culares, por los quales se ha contado y las competencias
de Juridicion y otros entre vos el dho custodia
y el dho mi Gou.or ha havido y ay, pretendiendo
Vos el dho Padre que en Virtud de las bulas
de Su Santidad Leon desimo, y Adriano Sexto

Chapter Two
1610-1821:

The Spanish

Santa Fe, New Mexico, was founded ten years before the Pilgrims landed at Plymouth Rock. That statement brings into perspective the age of the country's oldest capital, the home of the oldest public building, and many homes, churches, and other structures dating from the eighteenth and nineteenth centuries that are actively used today.

One can sit in the Santa Fe Plaza in front of the Palace of the Governors and not even realize that this is one of the most historic sites in America. Spanish, Pueblo Indian, Mexican, Anglo-American, and Confederate governments have ruled Santa Fe from the Palace since 1610.

Today, much is written about the three cultures of Santa Fe—Native American, Spanish, and Anglo. The land was Native American before it was Spanish, and Santa Fe was controlled for thirteen years (1680-93) by Native Americans, but it is the Spanish influence that is most pervasive.

One can see that influence in the architecture (albeit combined with Native American styles), the language, and the faces of many Santa Feans.

On page 15 is a chart that traces one family from the mid-1600s to the present day, one of many such families that can trace its ancestry to the soldiers and colonists who arrived in Santa Fe in the seventeenth century.

Seventy years after the Spanish first entered, explored, and then occupied much of present-day New Mexico, the capital of Nuevo Mejico was established by Don Pedro de Peralta in Santa Fe. Peralta was the second governor of New Mexico.

His predecessor, Juan de Oñate, had settled this northern frontier in 1598, along with Franciscan friars, soldiers, and colonists he had brought with him from Mexico. The Spanish crown had given him a contract to colonize the area.

As befitted a Spanish town, a plaza was laid out in Santa Fe (it originally extended to what is now St. Francis Cathedral on the east side), and El Palacio de Los Gobernadores ("the Palace of the Governors") was built on the north. The Palace today serves as the main unit of the Museum of New Mexico.

No other building remains from those early years, although underneath the present buildings, sidewalks, streets, and parks are probably buried many artifacts from that early period.

Colonists came from present-day Mexico to settle along the few rivers of New Mexico. Their government was in Santa Fe.

Church and state relations were never close during this period (1610-80), and accusations were tossed back and forth between governors and church officials.

The Spanish Inquisition was a part of Santa Fe life for many Spanish settlers during the seventeenth and part of the eighteenth centuries. More than one governor of that period was accused of crimes by the Holy Office of the Inquisition; some were arrested, imprisoned (in their own Palace of the Governors), and taken to Mexico for trial.

One such governor, Don Fernando López de

1621 Document

The earliest document in existence from the Spanish period in Santa Fe is this one, written in 1621. It consists of instructions from the Royal Audiencia in Mexico to

Fray Estéban de Perea concerning conversion of the Indians of New Mexico.

Photo courtesy of the State Records Center and Archives, Series II

Mendizábal (1656-61), died in prison, but was later absolved of his "crimes" by the Inquisiton. He had been accused of practicing Judaism. Evidence was introduced that he and his wife bathed on Friday nights, at which time she shut herself up in her bedroom for her ablutions.

The Pueblo Indians were sometimes underpaid for their tasks (their labor built the Palace and other early Santa Fe buildings), and, despite Spanish laws, some Spaniards abused and mistreated them. They attempted several times in the seventeenth century to get rid of the Spanish; unsuccessful revolts in some pueblos were staged in 1640, circa 1668, circa 1670, and 1675.

Finally, in 1680, through a strong alliance of the Pueblos (later joined by the Apaches), a revolt was carried out. It began on Saturday, August 10, 1680, on the Feast of San Lorenzo. By August 15, Santa Fe was under siege. The capital was filled by that time with refugees from La Cañada, a settlement north of Santa Fe and almost as old, and from the Cerrillos district, to the southeast. The flight of the Spaniards and the Indians loyal to them began from Santa Fe on August 21.

Refugees from the Rio Abajo area (in the vicinity of the present-day Albuquerque) were met by the Santa Fe contingent south of Socorro, and, together, they retreated to El Paso del Norte, in the area of today's El Paso, Texas, and Ciudad Juárez, Mexico.

Attempts were made to reconquer Santa Fe and the rest of northern New Mexico, but none was successful until Don Diego deVargas accomplished it in 1693. In September 1692 deVargas and his men peacefully made a reconnaissance of the area. In December 1693 he returned with a party of soldiers, colonists, and friars, and, after a battle, Santa Fe was once again in Spanish hands.

After the reconquest, more and more Spanish settlers came to Santa Fe and northern New Mexico. The need for land led to the grant system, whereby individuals and groups of heads of families were given tracts of land. Disputes over the ownership of these grants have found their way into the courtrooms over succeeding generations. The land-grant question was settled, as far as the courts were concerned, in 1903, but a legacy of bitterness has remained for many individuals and families.

The Pueblo Indians and Spanish lived in relative harmony after the Reconquest, but attacks from Navajos and Apaches (and, occasionally, from Utes and Comanches) remained a concern for Santa Fe residents well into the nineteenth century. Santa Fe itself was comparatively safe; the other towns and outlying settlements in the northern part of New Mexico were most subject to attack.

Not only the Palace of the Governors and the Plaza remain from the Spanish years. *La Conquistadora,* the small statue that was taken with the fleeing Santa Feans in 1680, and returned with them in 1693, rests in her chapel within St. Francis Cathedral. Many residents honor her throughout the year (she is the patron saint of New Mexico and a symbol of Hispanic unity), and the city is reminded of her through annual celebrations.

In 1712, in commemoration of the events of 1692, it was announced by the municipal authorities that an annual fiesta would be held every September. Today it is the chief celebration of the city, although it was not observed during most of the years since its founding.

Foreigners were excluded from New Mexico, although a few French or Anglo-American traders made their way in. They did so at their own risk. Those caught were taken first to Santa Fe, and then to Mexico. Spain's xenophobia increased when Napoleon Bonaparte sold the vast Louisiana area to the United States in 1803. It only brought the Anglo-Americans that much closer.

Changes were frequent during the Napoleonic period and the revolutionary era of 1810-15. Events in Santa Fe were quiet compared to the turbulence going on in Mexico, but, when the revolt against the Spanish finally took hold, Santa Fe found itself a part of the Republic of Mexico and no longer an outpost of the vast Spanish empire that had encompassed so many millions of square miles of the globe.

Santa Fe was, however, still on the northern frontier, and communication with Mexico City was infrequent and slow.

Pueblo Revolt Poster

The 300th anniversary of the Pueblo Revolt, celebrated in 1980, included a reenactment of the run from one pueblo to another to alert the inhabitants to the exact date of the revolt. Knotted cords were used as a code by the runners to reveal to the leaders what day to begin the uprising. The official tricentennial poster by Tommy Edward Montoya (Than Tśáy-ta') of San Juan Pueblo is titled, Thanks to Mother Earth.

Photo courtesy of the All-Indian Pueblo Council Tricentennial Commission and Herman Agoyo

1680 PUEBLO REVOLT 1980

TRICENTENNIAL COMMEMORATION NEW MEXICO.

13

Ortiz y Pino

Queen Isabella of Spain financed the expedition of the Italian Christopher Columbus, so it seemed only fitting that Spanish explorers and colonists should be among the first to visit and settle the New World.

Exactly 200 years after Columbus's discovery of the Western Hemisphere, a Spanish captain and governor, Don Diego deVargas, set out from El Paso del Norte to reconnoiter the former Spanish possession of New Mexico with its capital at Santa Fe.

After his successful reconquest, the capital was once again inhabited by Spanish families, some of whom had lived there before the Pueblo Revolt of 1680.

In his book *Origins of New Mexico Families* New Mexico historian Fray Angelico Chávez, himself a descendant of some of the first colonists to Santa Fe, lists five groups of such colonists to come with or soon follow deVargas in the 1690s.

1. The "native New Mexicans," those returning to Santa Fe after their thirteen-year exile in El Paso del Norte, included families named Archuleta, Baca, Chavez, Lucero, and Montoya, names very evident in Santa Fe today.

2. Three of the soldiers from Spain remained to establish families in the reconquered capital; they were named Paéz Hurtado, Fernandez de la Pedrera, and Roybal.

3. The viceroy selected sixty-seven families from the valley of Mexico to move to New Mexico and help colonize it. Those "Españoles Mexicanos" (not all made it to their new home) included the names Aragón, Medina, Ortiz, and Quintana. Some of them established themselves in the new villa of Santa Cruz de la Cañada in March 1695, and others arrived in Santa Fe in late June 1694.

4. Juan Paéz Hurtado, on occasion acting governor of New Mexico at later dates, recruited families from the mining community of Zacotecas, Mexico; these families arrived in Santa Fe in May 1695.

5. A few families living in El Paso del Norte, then a part of New Mexico, also joined the other colonists in settling the post-Pueblo Revolt Santa Fe. Some of them had been born in El Paso del Norte. This fifth group included families named Padilla and Perea.

On these pages you will find a family chart showing

It is not known when or where this statue was made, but, as Our Lady of the Assumption, she left Mexico City in 1625 with Fray Alonso de Benavides, a Franciscan friar, delegate of the Holy Office and head of the missions of New Mexico.

During the Pueblo Revolt in 1680, she was one of the objects taken from Santa Fe by the fleeing Spanish. She became famous in 1693 when the reconquering Spanish gave her credit for making it possible to defeat the Pueblo Indian defenders of

Santa Fe, and she was renamed "La Conquistadora." deVargas wrote to his superior, the viceroy, that it was his and his soldiers' wishes to build a church, setting up in it "the patroness of the said kingdom and villa, who is the one that was saved from the fury of the savages, her title being Our Lady of the Conquest" (Chavez, La Conquistadora).

The La Conquistadora chapel that is found today in St. Francis Cathedral was at one time a part of La Parroquia, the predecessor to the cathedral, built in the early 1700s on the site of an earlier church constructed by Fray Alonso.

La Conquistadora has undergone many changes in dress and has even been physically altered (in the late 1700s, the base of the statue was sawed off and part of her right knee was cut off to fit her into a glass box), but she has remained a strong symbol of Spanish heritage and religious fervor in Santa Fe. Today, she is carried in an annual procession from the St. Francis Cathedral to Rosario Chapel, the site of deVargas's camp when he was beginning the reconquest of Santa Fe in 1693. Tyler Dingee captured her here in a 1951 pose in her chapel at the cathedral.

Photo courtesy of the Museum of New Mexico (negative no. 73832)

La Conquistadora

twelve generations of the Ortiz y Pino family, one of the most prominent families associated with Santa Fe and northern New Mexico. Captain Nicolás Ortiz I and his wife, Doña Mariana Coronado, moved to Santa Fe in 1693.

Nicolás was born in Mexico City in 1653 and his wife, the daughter of Francisco Hernández of Jimiquilpa, Mexico, was born in 1665, probably in Jimiquilpa. (Doña Mariana's name appears variously as María Ana deVargas Barba Coronado and Doña Mariana Coronado, while her husband is shown on the colonists' list as "Ortiis.")

Many members of the Ortiz y Pino family have been important to New Mexico and Santa Fe history. While not all of those listed on the accompanying chart

were born in or even lived in Santa Fe, it is interesting to note that many of them did, including the earlier and later generations. Several other families could have been chosen who would have produced a similar chart, one that traced directly from the seventeenth-century Spanish settlers of Santa Fe to late twentieth-century schoolchildren of the same municipality.

Not all members of the family nor all spouses are shown for each generation because of a lack of space, but the chart will give an indication of the importance of this family over several centuries, and it shows the descendancy from the early colonists to the present day.

Because of the number of intermarriages between the various Spanish colonial families, many others in Santa Fe today can claim relatives in this chart.

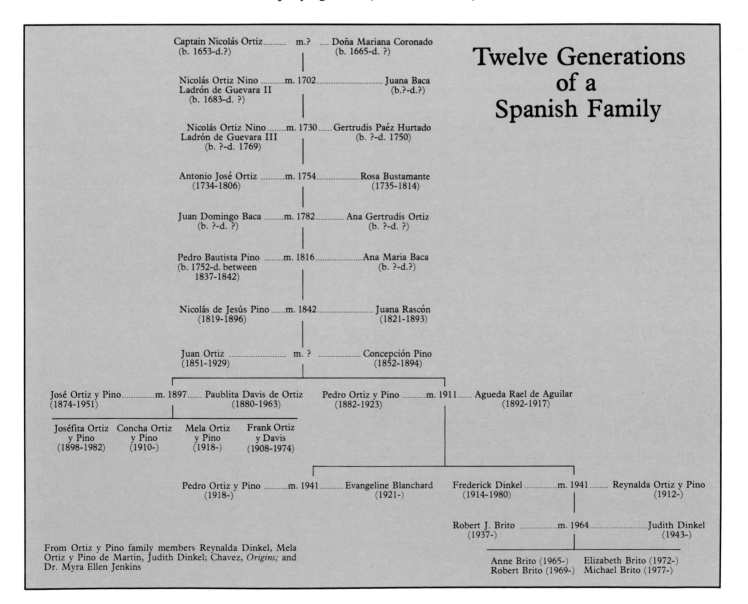

Captain Nicolás Ortiz.......... m.? .... Doña Mariana Coronado
(b. 1653-d.?)   (b. 1665-d. ?)

Nicolás Ortiz Nino ....m. 1702......................... Juana Baca
Ladrón de Guevara II   (b.?-d.?)
(b. 1683-d. ?)

Nicolás Ortiz Nino ......m. 1730......Gertrudis Paéz Hurtado
Ladrón de Guevara III   (b. ?-d. 1750)
(b. ?-d. 1769)

Antonio José Ortiz ....m. 1754................Rosa Bustamante
(1734-1806)   (1735-1814)

Juan Domingo Baca ....m. 1782............ Ana Gertrudis Ortiz
(b. ?-d. ?)   (b. ?-d. ?)

Pedro Bautista Pino ......m. 1816.................Ana Maria Baca
(b. 1752-d. between   (b. ?-d.?)
1837-1842)

Nicolás de Jesús Pino ......m. 1842.....................Juana Rascón
(1819-1896)   (1821-1893)

Juan Ortiz .... m. ? .... Concepción Pino
(1851-1929)   (1852-1894)

José Ortiz y Pino............m. 1897...... Paublita Davis de Ortiz   Pedro Ortiz y Pino ....m. 1911...... Agueda Rael de Aguilar
(1874-1951)   (1880-1963)   (1882-1923)   (1892-1917)

Joséfita Ortiz Concha Ortiz Mela Ortiz Frank Ortiz
y Pino   y Pino   y Pino   y Davis
(1898-1982)   (1910-)   (1918-)   (1908-1974)

Pedro Ortiz y Pino ....m. 1941........Evangeline Blanchard   Frederick Dinkel ....m. 1941....... Reynalda Ortiz y Pino
(1918-)   (1921-)   (1914-1980)   (1912-)

Robert J. Brito ....m. 1964....................Judith Dinkel
(1937-)   (1943-)

From Ortiz y Pino family members Reynalda Dinkel, Mela Ortiz y Pino de Martin, Judith Dinkel; Chavez, *Origins;* and Dr. Myra Ellen Jenkins

Anne Brito (1965-) Elizabeth Brito (1972-)
Robert Brito (1969-) Michael Brito (1977-)

Twelve Generations of a Spanish Family

deVargas Painting

Don Diego deVargas Zapata y Lujan Ponce de León, Marqués de la Nava de Brazinas, was successful in his reconquest of New Mexico in 1692-93. deVargas first entered the Pueblo Indian-controlled Santa Fe in 1692 and met no resistance, but had to do bloody battle in December 1693 to reconquer the capital. This painting, a copy of one that hangs in Madrid, may be viewed in the Palace of the Governors, the same building he lived in and governed from (1693-97 and 1703-04)—and where he was imprisoned for three years as well.

Photo courtesy of the Museum of New Mexico (negative no. 11409)

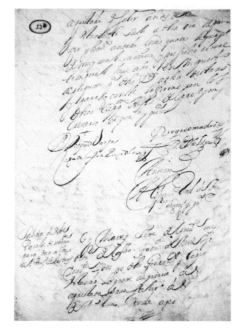

deVargas Journal

General deVargas kept this journal (the last page is shown here) during his travels throughout present-day New Mexico from his arrival in Santa Fe in September 1692 through 1696. In El Paso del Norte, shortly before he departed for the second time for Santa Fe, he stated that he had returned, "leaving the natives of the said kingdom completely and thoroughly reduced, surrendered and conquered for our holy faith and the royal crown," but he was to change his mind when, upon his return to Santa Fe, the Spanish had to fight with the Pueblo Indian occupants to retake the capital. Although Santa Fe was in Spanish hands relatively quickly, the Pueblo Indians in other parts of New Mexico were not finally subdued until 1696. From that time until the end of Spanish rule in the early nineteenth century, the Spanish and the Pueblo Indians lived in comparative peace.

Photo courtesy of the State Records Center and Archives, Spanish Archives of New Mexico, Series II

List of Colonists

The colonists who arrived in Santa Fe in 1693 (some of whom were returning to the capital they had fled thirteen years before) are listed in a lengthy document now in the New Mexico State Records Center and Archives in Santa Fe. Shown here is an entry for the Nicolás Ortiz family. Nicolás, his wife Doña Mariana Coronado, and children Josefa, Manuela, Nicolás II, Antonio, Luis, and Francisco received money from the government "in aid of the expenses necessary to provide for the journey." Nicolás "Ortiis" the elder is described as "40 years old, medium height, sharp nose, large eyes and bald."

Descendants of the seventeenth-century colonists make up many of the Spanish families in Santa Fe today, almost 300 years later. Through inter-marriage, most of those descendants are related to one another. (The Ortiz y Pino family history, page 15) begins with the elder Nicólas and his wife Doña Mariana and ends with some young Santa Feans who are direct descendants.)

Photo courtesy of the State Records Center and Archives, Spanish Archives of New Mexico, series II

Order to Celebrate Fiesta

On September 16, 1712, the Santa Fe ayuntamiento ("*town council*"), at a meeting at the house of the lieutenant governor, Captain General *Juan Paéz Hurtado*, declared that every September 14 thereafter a Fiesta would be held in Santa Fe to commemorate the reconquest of the capital by deVargas. The document calls for someone "*who may be fitting*" to give a sermon and be paid twenty-five pesos for it. (And another thirty pesos would be spent for the vespers, mass, and procession.) The celebration of the Fiesta did not take hold until the twentieth century, despite these early plans; today, it is a vital annual celebration in Santa Fe.

This 1712 document notes that the gathering for the announcement was made at Lieutenant Governor Paéz Hurtado's house because the houses of the other men involved were unavailable due to the continuous rains and heavy thunderstorms for the three preceding days. Concern for water has always been a topic of conversation in Santa Fe, but rarely has an excess of it been discussed.

Photo courtesy of the State Records Center and Archives, Spanish Archives of New Mexico, series I, no. 179

Rawhide Chest

Rawhide chests were one means of conveying goods in the busy trade between Santa Fe and Chihuahua, Mexico. Such commerce went on for the more than two centuries of Spanish rule and continued under the Mexican and American governments. It was rivaled in the nineteenth century by the busy traffic found on the Santa Fe Trail (Santa Fe to Independence, Missouri). This particular chest was used in the eighteenth century.

Photo courtesy of the State Records Center and Archives, Department of Development Collection

Reredos, Guadalupe

This oil-on-canvas reredos ("altar screen") in Our Lady of Guadalupe Church was painted by José de Alzibar in 1783 in Mexico and brought to Santa Fe in the same year, rolled up in an oxcart. It may have been given to the church by Antonio José Ortiz and his wife. It is not known the exact year the church was built. (It was licensed in 1795.) The reredos was cleaned and restored in the 1970s when the church itself was partially returned to an eighteenth-century appearance, after having gone through many architectural styles, not unlike many other older buildings in Santa Fe. Alongside the church is Agua Fria Street, once known as El Camino Real ("the royal road") from Mexico City to Santa Fe.

Photo courtesy of the State Records Center and Archives, Historic Santa Fe Foundation Collection

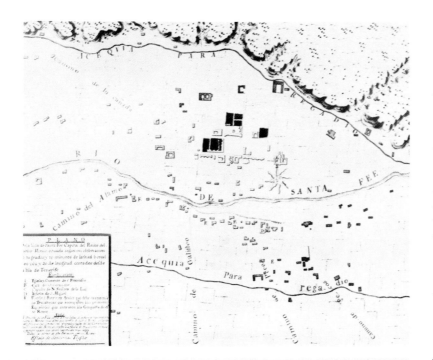

Urrutia Map

Second Lieutenant José Urrutia drew this map, the earliest known one of Santa Fe, in 1766-68, when he accompanied the Marqués de Rubi on an inspection tour of the presidios ("garrisons") of New Spain's northern frontiers. The original map is in the British Museum. Barbara Freire-Marreco, a lecturer at Oxford University, found the original in the museum and sent a copy to Jesse Nusbaum, a staff member of the School of American Archaeolgy (now the School of American Research), in 1912. He photographed the copy that year, the same one in which he took so many photographs of buildings and people in Santa Fe.

Photo courtesy of the Museum of New Mexico

Zebulon Pike

The Spanish authorities in Santa Fe and in Mexico City were fearful of the encroachment of the other European powers and the United States of America upon their territory. This xenophobia increased when the U.S. obtained neighboring Louisiana from Napoleon Bonaparte in 1803. The huge territory had recently belonged to Spain. Intruders caught in New Mexico were often imprisoned, although some French traders managed to buy and sell goods in Santa Fe (if the governor looked the other way) before the French were kicked out of North America.

Lieutenant Zebulon Pike, after whom Pike's Peak in Colorado is named, was one of several American trespassers who was brought to Santa Fe, then taken under military escort by Colonel (later Governor) Facundo Melgares to imprisonment in Chihuahua. Pike had been exploring the Louisiana Purchase in 1806 when he entered New Mexico. Although he claimed not to know he was out of U.S. territory, he had had to cross the Arkansas River to enter New Mexico—and he knew his boundaries well enough to know that.

Illman Brothers engraving; photo courtesy of the Museum of New Mexico (negative no. 7757)

Don Pedro Bautista Pino

Don Pedro Bautista Pino, at a meeting in the Palace of the Governors in Santa Fe in 1810, was selected to represent New Mexico at the cortes, *the Spanish representative body which assembled in Cadiz, Spain, during the Napoleonic occupation to draft a constitution for Spain.*

Pino arrived in Cadiz one year after leaving Santa Fe and presented to the other delegates a report on conditions in early nineteenth-century New Mexico titled La Exposición Sucinta y Sencilla de la Provincia del Nuevo México. *This report described the danger of possible aggression from a combination of Anglo-American and Native American forces from the Plains area; called for the establishment of more garrisons because of that danger; requested a separate bishopric, a college, and a system of schools for New Mexico; and the removal of the civil and criminal courts for New Mexico from Guadalajara to Chihuahua.*

Don Pedro was reelected representative to the 1820-21 cortes, *but the money appropriated for his travels did not reach him in time, so he could not attend.*

No portraits of Don Pedro are known to exist. Based on family photographs of his descendants, the artist Remor Ortiz drew this composite to represent Don Pedro Bautista Pino.

Composite courtesy of Mela Ortiz y Pino de Martin

Concepción Pino

Concepción "Conchita" Pino and her husband Juan Ortiz joined two prominent family lines when they married. Her mother, Juana Rascón, was the niece of Don Juan Rafael Rascón, the vicar general sent to New Mexico by the bishop of Durango.

Photo attributed to Dana Chase; courtesy of Mela Ortiz y Pino de Martin

Nicolás Pino and Juan Ortiz

Don Pedro's son, Don Nicolás de Jesus Pino (on the left in this composite photo), was born while Santa Fe was part of Spain and died only sixteen years before it became the capital of the forty-seventh state.

Don Nicolás was among those who plotted to overthrow the newly arrived U.S. government in 1846. One account states that the plotters were turned in to the new administration by Doña Tules, a colorful Santa Fe figure and the owner of at least one gambling salon in the capital at that time.

After the assassination of Governor Charles Bent by Mexican nationalists and Pueblo Indians in Taos, Don Nicolás

gave up all thoughts of overthrowing the government, and, in fact, swore his allegiance to it.

He pledged that his family would always serve in the government of New Mexico. Many have taken up that pledge. Don Nicolás himself served in the territorial legislature, as president of the council, as did his brothers Facundo and Miguel Estanislado. Don Nicolás's grandson, José Ortiz y Pino, also served in the New Mexico House of Representatives (1926-28). His daughter, Concha Ortiz y Pino de Kleven, continued the tradition by becoming not only a representative from 1936 to 1942, but served as party whip as well, the first woman to

hold that position in any state legislature. José Ortiz y Pino III, a great-grandson of Don Nicolás, was a member of the New Mexico Senate from 1964 to 1966.

Juan Ortiz (on the right), son-in-law of Don Nicolás Pino, brought the Ortiz name back into the family tree represented on these pages. He was descended from Captain Nicolás Ortiz. His ancestors were given the Ortiz mining grant at the foot of the Ortiz Mountains (also named for the family).

Pino photo attributed to Dana B. Chase; both photos courtesy of Mela Ortiz y Pino de Martin

José Ortiz y Pino

José Ortiz y Pino was a member of the first generation to use the name that showed the joining of the two prominent families, the Ortizes and the Pinos. His wife, Paublita Davis de Ortiz, was his first cousin. (His father, Juan Ortiz, was the brother of Paublita's mother, Josefa Ortiz y Ortiz. Her father, Captain Sylvestre Davis, was a geologist from a well-known Massachusetts family and the first Yankee in the family.)

José Ortiz y Pino served as a member of the New Mexico House of Representatives from 1926 to 1928. He was a prominent New Mexican and did much to preserve the Spanish way of life in New Mexico. He had a strong devotion to the government, the Catholic church, and his family, a trait shared by other members of the extensive Ortiz y Pino family.

Photo courtesy of Mela Ortiz y Pino de Martin

Concha Ortiz y Pino de Kleven

Concha Ortiz y Pino de Kleven carried on her great-grandfather Don Nicolás Pino's pledge by becoming a member of the New Mexico state legislature in the 1930s and by serving as party whip at that time for the majority party, the Democrats.

Photo by Robert Martin

Reynalda Dinkel

In 1975 two of Don Pedro's great-great-granddaughters, Reynalda Dinkel, pictured here, and her first cousin, Concha Ortiz y Pino de Kleven, represented the family and New Mexico at a ceremony at the San Felipe de Neri Church in Cadiz, Spain, where they unveiled a plaque commemorating Don Pedro and his work with the Spanish cortes in 1812. Proclamations issued by Santa Fe Mayor Joseph Valdes, Archbishop Roberto Sanchez, and New Mexico Governor Jerry Apodaca were presented to the Spanish government.

Photo by Robert Martin

Pedro and Agueda Wedding

Pedro Ortiz y Pino married Agueda Rael de Aguilar in 1911. The marriage produced several children, one of whom was Reynalda Ortiz y Pino, the grandmother of the four Brito children (below).

Photo courtesy of Reynalda Dinkel

Brito Children

The Brito children, left to right, Elizabeth, Michael, Anne and Robert, of Santa Fe, are the great-great-great-great-great-great-great-great-grandchildren of Captain Nicolás Ortiz and Doña Mariana Coronado, who moved to Santa Fe in 1693 with their six children. One of them, Nicolás, was ten years old at the time, the same age as Elizabeth in this photo.

Photo by John Sherman

Drawing of Trail

The entrance of the caravan into Santa Fe is portrayed in this drawing. The children see a group of wagons and the U.S. flag in the distance. In the wagons would be goods for sale in Santa Fe or destined for points further into Mexico, such as Chihuahua.

Photo courtesy of the Museum of New Mexico

Chapter Three
1821-1846:

The Mexican Interlude

Santa Fe joined many other Spanish communities of the Western Hemisphere in the early nineteenth century when it, too, became independent of the mother country.

The residents of Santa Fe were not clamoring or plotting the independence of their capital and its territory like so many others were; the cause of independence was fought entirely in Mexico.

Although the Spanish governor, Facundo Melgares, became the Mexican governor in a smooth transition, one remarkable change did take place when an independent Mexico assumed power: No longer were the borders closed to outside trade. In fact, such trade was encouraged and, for the first time, wagonloads of goods went back and forth between Santa Fe and the United States on a regular, profitable basis. The Santa Fe Trail (Santa Fe to Independence, Missouri) was begun when William Becknell and other Americans arrived in November 1821 with a pack train of goods for sale. Traders on both sides of the border took advantage of the sudden transformation in government policy and braved weather, terrain, and hostile Indians to take goods to and from Santa Fe.

The already existing, lucrative trail from Santa Fe almost straight south to Chihuahua did not suffer. It continued to be a source of profit for many hardy persons, and some of the U.S. traders who brought their goods as far as Santa Fe continued onwards to Chihuahua. Santa Fe served as the hub for these activities and further increased in importance when the Spanish Trail (Santa Fe-Los Angeles) opened in 1829-30.

Arriving at this time in the Santa Fe area were the so-called "mountain men," the trappers of U.S. and sometimes French-Canadian descent, to trap beavers in New Mexico waters. Many of them (and many traders) married into Spanish families, became naturalized citizens, and even held political office.

Journalism came to Santa Fe near the end of the Mexican period when two newspapers, *La Verdad* ("The Truth") and *El Payo de Nuevo Mejico* ("The Peasant of New Mexico"), were published briefly in 1844-45 by the government. They were printed on a press that had been brought over the Santa Fe Trail in 1834 by Josiah Gregg, later the author of *Commerce on the Prairies,* a popular description of life in the Southwest and on the Santa Fe Trail. By the time the two newspapers were printed, the press was owned by Padre Martinez of Taos, a colorful New Mexican, who rented it to the authorities.

In 1836 a new administration in Mexico City changed the system of government in Mexico from states and territories to departments. This proved unpopular with the residents of northern New Mexico. That dislike, coupled with a strong distaste for the new governor, Albino Pérez, because he was not a native New Mexican and had enforced the new tax laws, brought about a revolution. It began in the Chimayó-Santa Cruz de la Cañada area north of Santa Fe, and Pérez and his cabinet, unable to put the revolt down, fled the capital. Pérez was caught and assassinated near Agua Fria, south of town.

A former governor, Manuel Armijo, who dominated New Mexico politics during the Mexican period, was sent to Santa Fe to recapture the government. The rebels' replacement for Pérez had been José Gonzalez, a *genizaro* from Ranchos de Taos. (A *genizaro* was an Indian who was living outside his/her own ethnic group, living in an "Europeanized status.") Gonzales was killed, as were the other leaders of the short-lived revolt.

Armijo again became governor and remained so until the arrival of the Anglo-Americans in 1846 (with the exception of about two years, 1843-45, when he was removed).

In 1841 Santa Fe was threatened by the young, independent Republic of Texas when troops from there were sent to take over the capital—and the trade caravans on the Santa Fe Trail. The threat was removed when Armijo's troops took prisoner those of the forces that had reached New Mexico; the survivors were taken to Mexico City in chains. (A little more than twenty years later, Texas Confederates would make it to Santa Fe and control it for a brief period.)

In 1846 President James Polk got Congress to declare war against Mexico in his attempts to expand the boundaries of the United States. Brigadier-General Stephen Watts Kearny led his "Army of the West" from Leavenworth, Missouri, to Bent's Fort on the Arkansas River in what is now Colorado. There he announced that he would occupy New Mexico and that resistance was useless. One of the American traders on the Independence-Santa Fe-Chihuahua trade had been James Magoffin, married to Doña Maria Gertrudes Valdez de

Beremende, of a prominent Chihuahua family, and a cousin of Governor Manuel Armijo.

This connection proved extremely important in 1846 when Magoffin, accompanied by a dozen soldiers from Kearny's camp at Bent's Fort under Philip St. George Cooke, came to Santa Fe with a white truce flag to negotiate with Armijo. The extent of the negotiations has never been proved, but Armijo fled when Kearny approached from Apache Cañon, about ten miles east of Santa Fe. On August 18, 1846, Kearny entered Santa Fe and the acting governor, Juan Bautista Vigil y Alarid, surrendered at the Palace of the Governors. The U.S. flag was raised in the Plaza.

The Santa Feans had been very afraid of Kearny and his men. They had been told that the men would destroy the Catholic faith, plunder the homes, and dishonor the women. Santa Fe town officials debated whether or not to tear down all the churches to prevent them from becoming military barracks and being otherwise desecrated. Some of the Americans living in Santa Fe dissuaded them, and the churches (three of which are still in use today) were saved.

The brisk, profitable trade that had become so well established during the twenty-five years of Mexican rule continued to entice men from the eastern United States to Santa Fe to establish retail and wholesale businesses that would cater to individuals and companies, in time, over a large part of the United States.

Canteen

The hardships of the Santa Fe Trail were offset by the profits to be made in trading goods between the Mexican republic and the United States. Beginning in Independence, Missouri, and ending in Santa Fe (and, later, continuing to Chihuahua, Mexico), the trail brought not only trade. It also made many Anglo-Americans aware of Santa Fe and the territory of New Mexico. The trail opened the route for conquest.

Photo courtesy of the State Records Center and Archives, Department of Development Collection

Bulto

This bulto ("free-standing statue") of Santa Librada, carved circa 1830, is typical of religious art made in Santa Fe during the Spanish and Mexican periods. The scarcity of religious images and ornaments in the churches gave rise to wood carvings and paintings on wood. The carving of wooden statues of saints continues today: The santero ("maker of images of saints") makes images very similar to those made generations ago. In today's annual summertime Spanish Market on the Santa Fe Plaza, art by dozens of carvers and painters is very popular.

Photo by Arthur Taylor; courtesy of the Museum of New Mexico (negative no. 74491)

Condé Document

Alejo García Condé, Comandante General in Mexico, announced in this August 24, 1821, document to the governor of New Mexico, Facundo Melgares, who had the distinction of being governor under the Spanish and then under the Mexicans, that Mexico was now independent from Spain. General Agustín de Iturbide, one of the revolution's leaders, had declared himself Emperor of Mexico the next year, but he was removed by a revolution one year after that. Only one man, Guadalupe Victoria, assumed and held office for a full term in the twenty-five years that Santa Fe was a part of an independent Mexico. The rest of the time, revolution, unrest, civil war, and a continual change of government characterized the Mexican period.

Photo courtesy of the State Records Center and Archives, Mexican Archives of New Mexico

<table>
<tr><td>

AVISO.

HALLANDOME debidamente antorizado por el Presidente de los Estados Unidos de America, por la presente hago los Siguientes nombramientos para la gobernacion de Nuevo Mejico, Territorio de los Estados Unidos.

Los Empleados asi nombrados seran obedecidos y respetados segun corresponde.

CARLOS BENT Será GOBERNADOR,
Donaciano Vigil " Secretario del Territorio,
Ricardo Dallam " Esherif mayor (alguacil
Francisco P. Blair " Promotor fiscal, [mayor)
Carlos Blummer " " Tesorero
Eugenio Leitensdorfer " Yntendente de cuentas públicas,
Joab Houghton, Antonio José Otero y Carlos Braubien seran Jués de la Suprema Corte de Justicia y cada uno en su Districto sqra jues de cir cuito.

Dado en Santa Fé capital del terri de Nuevo Mejico este dia á 22 de de Setiembre 1846, y el 71 ° de la Indepencia de los Estados Unidos·
S. W KEARNY,
General de Brigada
del Egercito de los E. Unidos.

</td><td>

NOTICE.

BEING duly authorized by the President of the United States of America, I hereby make the following appointments for the Government of New Mexico, a territory of the United States.

The officers thus appointed will be obeyed and respected accordingly·

CHARLES BENT to be Governor.
Donaciano Vigil " Sec. of Territory.
Richard Dallam " Marshall
Francis P Blair " U.S.D. A y
Charles Blummer " Treasurer.
Eugene Leitensdorfer " Aud. of Pub. Acc.
Joal Houghton, Antonio José Otero, Charles Beaubien to be Judges of "the Superior Court."

Given at Santa Fe, the Capitol of the Territory of New Mexico, this 22d day of September 1846 and in the 71st year of the Independence of the United States.

S. W. KEARNY,
Brig. General
U. S. Army.

</td></tr>
</table>

Pérez Rock

Kearny Proclamation

In 1846 Brigadier-General Stephen Watts Kearny entered Santa Fe and became the representative of the fourth power to occupy the capital. Rumors had been flying as to the intentions of the invaders. Many believed their daughters, their possessions, and their religion would not be safe. Kearny acted quickly— through announcements at meetings of Santa Feans, and the actions of the soldiers under his strict command—to dispel these notions. Santa Fe had become a U.S. possession.

Photo courtesy of the State Records Center and Archives, Territorial Archives of New Mexico

Changes in the form of government and an enforcement of unpopular laws caused many citizens to take part in what came to be called the Chimayó Rebellion in 1837. A fleeing Governor Albino Pérez was assassinated south of Santa Fe, near the village of Agua Fria. Manuel Armijo, governor before and after Pérez, had those responsible executed in the Santa Fe Plaza. This rock monument was placed on the site where Pérez was assassinated, but was moved to the patio of the Palace of the Governors in 1968 because of vandalism.

Photo courtesy of the State Records Center and Archives, Historic Santa Fe Foundation Collection

Manuel Armijo

General Manuel Armijo, often more style than substance, more interested in lining his own pockets than in governing well, was, nonetheless, an important influence on New Mexico during the Mexican period. His terms of office were marked by a strong interest in a flourishing trade between Mexico and the United States, with Santa Fe as the central figure in an activity amounting to millions of dollars. As the Americans approached Santa Fe, Armijo, to the dismay of many of his officers (especially Diego Archuleta) fled south to Chihuahua. History believes he was bribed by James Magoffin, an American trader and relative by marriage. Certainly his sudden departure made it easier for the Americans to occupy Santa Fe.

Photo courtesy of the State Records Center and Archives

La Parroquia

The predecessor of today's St. Francis Cathedral, La Parroquia ("parish church"), greeted the Anglo-Americans who traversed the Santa Fe Trail in the Mexican period. This drawing, made in 1846, the year Mexico lost Santa Fe to the United States, shows Fort Marcy, built immediately by the U.S. Army, in the background. This church was almost not standing when the military arrived, however. Many Santa Feans, impressed with rumors of the anti-Catholic feelings of the invaders, were willing to tear down their churches rather than have them desecrated. In this drawing, Fort Marcy is shown closer to La Parroquia than it actually was.

Photo courtesy of the Museum of New Mexico (negative no. 21257)

Plaza Photo

In one of the earliest known photos of Santa Fe, a group of men stand at the southeast corner of the Plaza. The building in the middle is the Exchange Hotel, also known as LaFonda, and, after 1846, sometimes as the U.S. Hotel or United States Hotel. It was the forerunner of the present-day LaFonda. To the right is the Seligman & Clever store, where Geppetto's Restaurant is today, and an old residence is on the left-hand side. This picture, taken circa 1856, just after the Seligman & Clever store opened, shows Santa Fe as it looked to the weary travelers arriving from the long journey on the Santa Fe Trail.

Photo courtesy of the Museum of New Mexico (negative no. 10685)

Chapter Four
1846-1865:

The First Anglo-American Decades

Susan Shelby Magoffin arrived in Santa Fe two weeks after Brigadier-General Kearny. She was the bride of merchant Samuel Magoffin and the sister-in-law of James Magoffin, who had helped arrange the peaceful takeover of Santa Fe.

Susan Magoffin kept a diary during 1846-47; it was first published in 1926. The diary continues to be a popular book today because it gives the viewpoint of a young woman's travels over the Santa Fe Trail, her short time spent in Santa Fe, and her later travels in Mexico.

The Magoffin house was located, as she put it in her diary, "under the shadow" of the church (La Parroquia). She visited the Plaza early in her stay and described it in her entry for September 8, 1846: "On one side is the government house with a wide portal in front, opposite is a large church commenced by the predecessor of Gov. Armijo, 'tis not finished—and dwelling houses—the two remaining sides are fronted by stores and dwellings, all with portals, a shed the width of the pavements; it makes a fine walk—and in rainy weather there is no use for an umbrella" (Magoffin, *Down the Santa Fe Trail*). The church she mentioned was La Castrense, where Dunlap's department store is now located, and which contained the white stone *reredos* now in Cristo Rey Church.

Most of the inhabitants of Santa Fe accepted the overthrow of the Mexicans and the coming of the Anglo-Americans, but a number of prominent citizens plotted in December 1846 to get rid of the usurpers. The story goes that the following group of men met in Don Nicolás Pino's house to do their plotting and planning: Tomás Ortiz, Juan Felipe Ortiz, Diego Archuleta, Domingo C. de Baca, Miguel Pino, Nicolás Pino, Manuel Cháves, Santiago Armijo, Agustín Durán, Pablo Domínguez, José María Sánchez, Antonio María Trujillo, Santiago Martínez, Pascual Martínez, Vicente Martínez, Antonio Ortiz, Facundo Pino, Reverend Antonio José Martinez, and Father José Francisco Leyva. Many of these men were related by blood or marriage. Some were descendants of the original Spanish settlers, and their own descendants today are prominent citizens of Santa Fe. They felt strongly about surrendering to the Anglo-Americans, and sought, through their plotting, to restore the Mexican republic's sovereignty.

This plot might have been successful, according to one story, had it not been for Doña Tules (Gertrudis Barceló), a colorful Santa Fe figure. Tules ran one of the many gambling parlors in Santa Fe (on Burro Alley) where one could play the game of *monte*, enjoy a drink, and otherwise have a good time. She had become friends with the Americans and had even lent the garrison money. (As part of her repayment, she was escorted to a ball by an American officer, much to the horror of the other women present.) The story has one of her servants, "a mulatto," hearing about the plot and reporting it to Tules who, in turn, quickly told the Americans. The plotters were arrested and jailed. (Many of the men on this list later served with distinction in the New Mexico territorial legislature and in other capacities in the government.)

In January 1847 a much more serious threat to the new government appeared: In Taos, Charles Bent, recently appointed governor by Kearny, was killed, along with other Anglos and Hispanics loyal to the Anglo-American rulers. Colonel Sterling Price with U.S. troops, and Ceran St. Vrain with a "mountain man" militia company (enlisted in Santa Fe) marched north and suppressed the revolt. It was at this time that men like Nicolás Pino swore allegiance to the new government (the very one they had tried to overthrow themselves only weeks before) and helped bring about a more peaceful transition from Mexican to Anglo-American administrations.

Three years after the takeover of Santa Fe, the *New Mexican,* the Santa Fe newspaper which calls itself "the oldest newspaper in the West" first appeared on November 28, 1849, succeeding the earlier *Santa Fe Republican.*

Kearny had declared New Mexico a territory, but Congress repudiated his declaration (it was not his to make, it was decided), and delayed giving the newly acquired area that status until 1850, the same year that statehood became an issue. (A constitutional convention adopted that plan, but Congress chose to ignore it, something it would do several times before New Mexico became a state in 1912.)

A cleric arrived in Santa Fe in 1851 who left a mark upon the town that is still felt today. Jean Baptiste Lamy, French-born, stubborn, and determined to run the church the way he felt it should be run, is yet a controversial figure. He was thinly disguised as the central figure in Willa Cather's *Death Comes for the Archbishop,* but other writers have not dealt so gently with him. He reformed a decadent church, some feel; others complain about his insensitive, thick-headed devotion to a Franco-Anglo church in a Hispanic land.

Today, if one looks at his statue in front of St. Francis Cathedral, one can see his chin protruding from a face that looks dourly down on passersby, and one can imagine the wrath that might have been encountered in a struggle with him for power and influence.

Through his efforts, Santa Fe today has St. Vincent Hospital, established by the Sisters of Charity; St. Francis Cathedral, built in the Romanesque style common to his native France; Loretto Chapel, also built in a French style for the Sisters of Loretto, and their institution, Loretto Academy for Girls; St. Michael's High School and the College of Santa Fe, both outgrowths of the old St. Michael's College, a Christian Brothers institution. The resort Bishop's Lodge was built around the chapel and house to which he retired just north of Santa Fe.

The clergy Lamy brought to Santa Fe were not only foreign to the area, but were French, Belgian, and Italian. He and many of his subordinates seemed tireless, always traveling about the area seeking converts and encouraging the "correct" practice of Catholicism.

The era of foreign-born merchants dominating the commerce of Santa Fe began when Solomon Jacob Spiegelberg arrived with the U.S. Army in 1846. During the next decade and a half, his five brothers, Levi, Elias, Emanuel, Lehman, and Willi, also moved to Santa Fe. They operated a store on the south side of the Plaza and were also involved in many other business ventures. Another early merchant was Sigmund Seligman who formed a partnership in 1856 with Charles P. Clever. Both were Germans. Later, Sigmund's brother Bernard arrived from Frankfurt-am-Main, where he had worked with the Rothschilds, and the two formed Seligman Brothers, wholesale and retail dry goods merchants. The influx of Anglo-Americans and European-born church and business people had begun in earnest.

Doña Tules

This uncomplimentary portrait of Doña Tules that appeared in Harper's Monthly Magazine *for April 1854 was no doubt influenced by the "shocking" habit of some Hispanic women in Santa Fe to smoke cigarillos, something Anglo-American women rarely did, even in private. The cultural clash of Anglo-American and Hispanic-American had begun. Religions, languages, dress, customs, and physical appearances were often different—and still are. Had it not been for this sorry-looking woman, so the story goes, the plot against the American government might have been successful, and many soldiers stationed in and near Santa Fe would have lost their lives or been imprisoned. President James Polk and many of his countrymen were determined, however, to have New Mexico as part of the United States, so a plot, even if successful, would not have kept the U.S. away for very long.*

Photo courtesy of the Museum of New Mexico (negative no. 50815)

LADY TULES.

Gilmore Map

This plan of Santa Fe was drawn up after the Anglo-American occupation, in 1846-47, by Lieutenant J. F. Gilmore of the U.S. Corps of Engineers. The "Governor's House" is the Palace of the Governors; the "road to Independence, Mo." is the Old Santa Fe Trail; the "road to Chihuahua" is Agua Fria Street. The "military church" on the south side of the Plaza was La Castrense.

Photo courtesy of the Museum of New Mexico

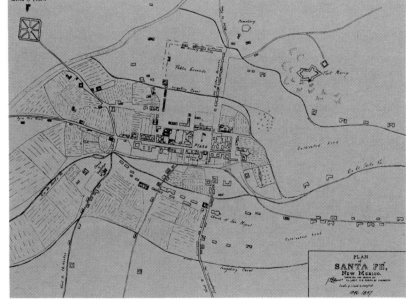

Kearny Portrait

Brigadier-General Stephen Watts Kearny declared New Mexico a territory upon his arrival in Santa Fe in 1846, but that status was not to be conferred by Congress until four years later, the same year the first call for statehood was made—and denied. In 1847 Kearny contracted yellow fever in Vera Cruz, Mexico, and died at the home of Major Meriwether Lewis Clark, son of William Clark of the Lewis and Clark expedition and a relative by marriage, in St. Louis in 1848.

Photo courtesy of the Museum of New Mexico (negative no. 9940)

Fort Marcy, Aerial View

Ridgework of Fort Marcy, hurriedly built in 1846 when the Anglo-Americans took Santa Fe, is still visible today. It was never garrisoned and never used for the defense of Santa Fe. (When the Confederates arrived in 1862, the troops had already fled eastward.) The house in the lower right-hand corner is the Santa Fe Girl's Club, formerly the residence of Major General Patrick Hurley. One of Santa Fe's two Crosses of the Martyrs is visible at the base of the fort.

Photo courtesy of the State Records Center and Archives, Historic Santa Fe Foundation Collection

Fireplace

During late twentieth-century renovations in the Palace of the Governors, this chimney of a territorial-style fireplace was discovered. It was built in the middle of the wall, departing from the Spanish tradition of a corner placement.

Photo courtesy of the Museum of New Mexico

Protestant Congregations

The first Protestant congregation in Santa Fe was a Baptist one formed in 1852. The Baptists withdrew at the beginning of the Civil War (just as many Santa Fe-based U.S. Army men resigned their commissions and went to fight for the Confederacy). Later, the Presbyterians built the church shown here. Between the departure of the Baptists and the organization of the Presbyterians, a "Protestant" church held services in the town. During that time (1862) the first Episcopal service in Santa Fe took place. This photo was taken circa 1879-81.

Photo by Ben Wittick; courtesy of the Museum of New Mexico, School of American Research Collections in the Museum of New Mexico (negative no. 15855)

Chapter Five
1865-1900:

Rapid Change

The Santa Fe of this period closely resembled other American towns, even though it had been a part of the United States for less than two decades by 1865.

Several changes dominated this period: the arrival of a great number of Anglo-Americans from the eastern United States, the coming of the railroad, the increasing use of the telegraph, and the slavish adoption of styles imported from east of the Mississippi, whether or not those styles fitted in.

The architecture is a case in point. Abandoning the traditional Native American-Spanish adobe materials and designs, many Santa Feans who could afford it built Victorian, Queen Anne, and other "Eastern" styles of houses and commercial buildings, even after these had ceased to be fashionable in the rest of the country.

The military began to be less of a force in Santa Fe as the need for soldiers in the area decreased; the civilian population grew as Easterners and Europeans continued to arrive. Not the least of these Europeans were some of the merchant families with names like Dendahl, Pflueger, Spitz, and Kaune, names still found in today's Santa Fe business community. (Earlier, other merchant families had preceded them, with surnames of Spiegelberg, Seligman, and Staab.) Many of the merchant families were German Jews who worked easily and mixed easily with the Spanish and Anglo families and with the Catholic and Protestant groups in Santa Fe.

One artist from outside the area is recorded as living for a time in Santa Fe during this period, foreshadowing the great numbers of artists who arrived in the first decades of the present century: J. H. Sharp arrived in 1883 and lived for a short time in Santa Fe and Taos before departing New Mexico.

Santa Fe was a popular topic in such national publications as *Frank Leslie's Weekly* and *Harper's Weekly*, whetting the appetites of schoolchildren and their parents. This coverage of the more exotic elements of Santa Fe and the Southwest in general helped bring about the interest of travelers in the area in succeeding decades.

Old Spanish families continued to honor family, church, and custom, and continued to intermarry with each other, and with others, particularly Catholics, who were not of Spanish heritage.

The Loretto Academy and St. Michael's College continued to provide an education for area Catholic girls and boys, respectively. St. Catherine Industrial Indian School for Boys, later coed St. Catherine Indian School; Ramona School; and the U.S. Indian School all served Pueblo and other Indians. Santa Fe High School began operating near the end of this period as Santa Fe's first public high school.

The Protestant church was represented by several denominations that arrived in Santa Fe after the largely Protestant United States military had set up Fort Marcy. The first Protestant church was a Baptist one, and the congregation that is now the oldest Protestant one in Santa Fe today came a short time later, the Presbyterians. The many denominations created a plethora of faiths in a town that had previously been

Fernando Delgado

Fernando Delgado (1824-75) was one of many Delgados to be prominent in Santa Fe in the eighteenth and nineteenth centuries. The Delgados had at one time owned a great deal of land in New Mexico. Fernando was the grandson of Captain Manuel Delgado, who enlisted in the Royal Army in Spain in 1776 and came to New Mexico two years later. Fernando was one of many in the family who was a merchant. One Delgado house remains in Santa Fe today, the Felipe B. Delgado house at 124 West Palace Avenue (now the home of New Mexico Banquest Corporation); others stood on the present site of the Lensic Theatre and where today's First National Bank has its main office, on the Plaza.

Photo courtesy of Anita Gonzales Thomas

host only to the Catholic church for centuries. The Roman Catholics, however, continued to provide the medical care and much of the education for the majority of Santa Feans, and the various churches—some centuries old—were dotted about the landscape and were already being considered "tourist attractions" by visitors and the Eastern press.

Santa Fe went through tremendous changes in these thirty-five years. Though some of those changes were to be reconsidered (and covered with adobe-brown stucco) in the next quarter century, much happened in Santa Fe and in the rest of the United States to bring Santa Fe to the national attention it has received throughout the twentieth century.

Cathedral and Plaza

The Plaza has always dominated Santa Fe. Though its appearance has constantly changed, it has remained a central part of the town. This photo, taken between 1866 and 1868, looked east. To the right is San Francisco Street leading to La Parroquia. (A clock was later installed on the front, near the top.) At this time, there were still residences on the Plaza, although businesses were more and more attracted to this part of Santa Fe.

Photo by Nicholas Brown; courtesy of the Museum of New Mexico (negative no. 38025)

Card With Trail's End

One of the many postcards touting Santa Fe carries the dubious claim that this well-drawn action scene was made from "an old original photograph." At any rate, the Santa Fe Trail did end at the Plaza where two businesses may be seen here: Seligman and Clever's and the Exchange Hotel.

Courtesy of Richard Levy and the Silver Sunbeam, Albuquerque

La Parroquia

La Parroquia was built circa 1710-12 and served as the main church for Santa Fe until Archbishop Lamy had St. Francis Cathedral constructed around it. (La Conquistadora chapel remains from the original structure.) This photo was taken by Nicholas Brown two years after the end of the Civil War, in 1867.

Courtesy of the Museum of New Mexico (negative no. 10059)

U.S. Courthouse

The present U.S. Courthouse on Federal Place, now on the National Register of Historic Places, seemed destined never to become a place to be included on anybody's register. The construction of this large stone building began in 1853 but was not finished until 1889.

U. S. Army Signal Corps photo; courtesy of the Museum of New Mexico (negative no. 10242)

New Mexican

The New Mexican *published out of this building, the Johnson Block, when this photo was taken in 1872 at the northeast corner of the Plaza. The First National Bank occupied rooms through the south door under the portal, and the* New Mexican *was found in rooms on the north side (on Palace Avenue). One entered T. B. Catron's law office from the south door by the lattice and went up to the second story. Around 1880 this building housed the post office below and a finishing school above. The structure was named after a James Johnson who came from Maryland to Santa Fe in 1852 and became a prominent citizen and merchant. Today, the Blatt Building (the Catron Block) occupies this space.*

Photo courtesy of the Museum of New Mexico (negative no. 10713)

Silver Spoons

These ornamental silver spoons, popular in New Mexico after the arrival of the railroad in 1880, are decorated with two of Santa Fe's most historic buildings, the Palace of the Governors and San Miguel Chapel. Both dates are incorrect. The Palace was built in 1610, and the chapel was constructed 100 years later.

Photo courtesy of the Museum of New Mexico

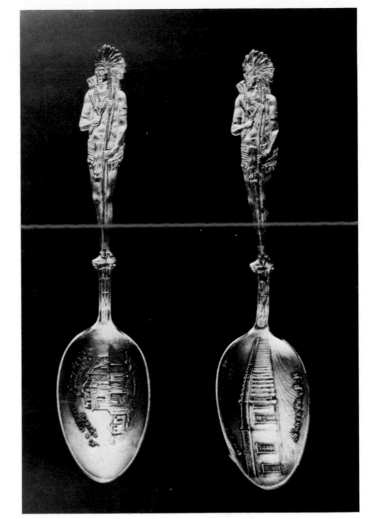

Corpus Christi

The Corpus Christi procession was, for a long time, a big social as well as religious event in Santa Fe. In this view of one such procession on San Francisco Street, La Parroquia can be seen in the background. Note the shops lining the southern tier of the Plaza. Those in the procession visited the family altars of the Delgado family on Delgado Street and of the Sena family on East Palace at Sena Plaza.

Courtesy of the State Records Center and Archives, Sylvia Loomis Collection

San Miguel Chapel

San Miguel Chapel was not built in 1582, as someone wrote on this 1880 photograph, but in 1710. It was constructed on the site of an earlier San Miguel Chapel that was destroyed in the 1680 Pueblo Revolt. Like many other buildings in Santa Fe, particularly the Palace of the Governors and Our Lady of Guadalupe Church, San Miguel has undergone many transformations, particularly exterior ones, in its appearance during its life time. In 1880 this small church served as part of the campus of St. Michael's College. Other buildings on that campus were to the east and south of this structure for more than a century.

Photo by Ben Wittick; courtesy of the Museum of New Mexico, School of American Research Collections in the Museum of New Mexico (negative no. 15856)

THE NEW CATHEDRAL.

Harper's

Harper's New Monthly Magazine of April 1880 touted "The New Cathedral" of Santa Fe in this illustration that shows the construction of St. Francis Cathedral around the existing La Parroquia. The older structure remained open for Mass during most of the construction, and it was not until the stone cathedral was built that the adobe La Parroquia was torn down. This was the first Roman Catholic cathedral to be built between Durango, Mexico, and St. Louis, Missouri. The 1869 cornerstone was stolen a few days after it was laid—and it was never seen again.

Photo courtesy of the Museum of New Mexico (negative no. 74486)

Guadalupe-1

The Santuario de Nuestra Señora de Guadalupe, Guadalupe Church, has undergone many changes since its origins, circa 1795. Photographer F. A. Nims showed it looking much like any church in the eastern part of the United States.

Photo courtesy of the Museum of New Mexico (negative no. 15145)

Guadalupe-2

Ben Wittick photographed Guadalupe Church before Nims did—when it looked like this (in 1880).

Photo courtesy of the Museum of New Mexico, School of American Research Collections in the Museum of New Mexico (negative no. 15847)

Guadalupe-3

The next year, Wittick photographed the interior of the church. Note how rough the flooring is. Today, Mass is rarely celebrated here, but art shows, concerts, and other community events of a cultural nature draw large crowds to the eighteenth-century sanctuary.

Photo courtesy of the Museum of New Mexico, School of American Research Collections in the Museum of New Mexico (negative no. 15848)

Calvary Band

The Ninth Cavalry Band, a group of black soldier-musicians under the direction of Professor Charles Spiegel, entertained Santa Feans on the Plaza in the last quarter of the nineteenth century. In this photo by Ben Wittick, the band posed in front of the gazebo on the Plaza in 1880.

Photo courtesy of the Museum of New Mexico, School of American Research Collections in the Museum of New Mexico (negative no. 50887)

Ulysses Simpson Grant

Inveterate nineteenth-century Santa Fe photographer Ben Wittick captured General U.S. Grant, his wife Julia, and children on their July 1880 visit to Santa Fe. While in town, the Grants stayed at one of the officer's residences in the Fort Marcy complex (at the corner of Marcy Street and Grant Avenue). The photo was probably taken on the porch of that house. Though a small town, Santa Fe played an important part in history that was disproportionate to its size, a feature that has characterized the place since its early seventeenth-century founding.

Photo courtesy of the Museum of New Mexico (negative no. 39392)

Hayes's Visit

President Rutherford B. Hayes spent the night in this house, the home of merchant Lehman Spiegelberg and his family, when he visited Santa Fe, also in 1880. It was originally owned by Civil War Governor Henry Connelly. Simon and Dora Nusbaum purchased the home and lived in it after the Spiegelbergs. The demolition of this house in late 1960 for a city parking lot (just south of the Berardinelli city building at Washington Avenue and Nusbaum Street) caused a great deal of controversy—and brought about the formation of the Historic Santa Fe Foundation, which works to preserve historic buildings.

Photo by Jesse Nusbaum; courtesy of the Museum of New Mexico (negative no. 61487)

Lew Wallace

Part of the epic Ben Hur was written by Territorial Governor Lew Wallace in the Palace of the Governors. (The book was written all over the state during his travels.) At one time, one room was designated the Ben Hur Room, although he did not use that room exclusively for his writing of the book. The December 22, 1880 New Mexican had this to say about it: "The first edition of Ben Hur has been exhausted, the entire five thousand copies composing the edition having been sold. The publishers, Harper Brothers, will begin to issue the second edition of five thousand copies immediately, having

many orders in advance for the second series. And the author smiles.'' Just days before, Governor Wallace had offered a $500 reward for the capture and delivery of Billy the Kid, a much more mundane— and threatening—matter for New Mexicans.

Photo courtesy of the State Records Center and Archives

Loretto Chapel

This 1881 view of Loretto Chapel reveals that the building looked much as it does today, yet the surroundings were drastically different. The chapel was built to be a part of the campus of the Loretto Academy for Girls, founded in 1853 by the Sisters of Loretto (brought to Santa Fe by Archbishop Lamy). The academy closed its doors in 1967, and St. Michael's High School began taking in girls at the same time. The chapel opened three years before this photograph was taken; it was not until 1888 that the three-foot-high iron statue of Our Lady of Lourdes was placed on the building's pinnacle.

Photo by Ben Wittick, courtesy of the Museum of New Mexico, School of American Research Collections in the Museum of New Mexico (negative no. 15854)

Sanatorium

Originally built to be a trade school, this building that became St. Vincent Sanatorium was begun in 1878 and completed in 1882 (and opened the next year). It was at one time the tallest building in Santa Fe. On the site of this building today is Marian Hall on East Palace Avenue. The sanatorium burnt down in 1896. Before the fire, the building had been used as a gathering spot where raffles were held, bands played, and classes were offered in music, painting, and drawing.

Photo courtesy of the Museum of New Mexico (negative no. 1379)

Abraham Staab

Abraham Staab, local merchant, built the Staab mansion on East Palace Avenue for his wife Julie in 1882. Her ghost, it is said, continues to inhabit the place, sharing it with Santa Feans and tourists who frequent the former mansion, now a part of La Posada, a local hotel. Whether one sees a ghost or not, one can view the fine woodwork and floors of the original house while on the way to dine in the Staab House restaurant in the hotel. Staab was one of many German-Jewish merchants to call Santa Fe home in the late nineteenth century.

Photo courtesy of the Museum of New Mexico (negative no. 11040)

Decoration Day

About three years after the Civil War, circa 1868, this black military band marched in a Decoration Day parade headed west down San Francisco Street. They paused near Herlow's Hotel to have this photo taken. Barely visible at the end of the street is La Parroquia.

Photo courtesy of the State Records Center and Archives, Betty Farrar collection

New Mexican, 1882

This front-page display of the New Mexican for July 4, 1882, was typical of the newspapers of that time. There was little relief for the eye in this paper, and advertisements competed with news stories for the front page.

Photo courtesy of the Museum of New Mexico

SANTA FE DAILY NEW MEXICAN.

VOLUME X—NUMBER 161   SANTA FE, NEW MEXICO, TUESDAY MORNING JULY 4, 1882.   PRICE, 5 CENTS

KALAKUA'S HOME.

James G. Blaine's Opinion Regarding The Commercial Importance Of Hawaii

Embodied In His Letter To The Resident United States Minister.

Lucky Baldwin Fails To Beat The Kentucky Horse At Chicago,

And The California Delegation Intend Walking Home.

Pueblo Again Distinguishes Herself By Another Murder.

Blaine on Hawaii

The Chicago Races.

Fatally Shot.

The English Parliament

Murdered.

Murder In Pueblo

Death By Lightning.

Floods at Manitou.

WASHINGTON.

Commodore Shufeldt Is Recalled from the Japanese Commission.

Nevada Wants To Increase Its Territory With A Slice Of California.

General Gossip.

English Markets.

Turkey Will Do Nothing

Pugilistic

German Finances

An Oregon Fire.

Strikers Struck

Waked Out

FORTY-SEVENTH CONGRESS

SENATE.

HOUSE.

FOREIGN FLASHES.

Stock Quotations.

New York, July 3.

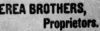

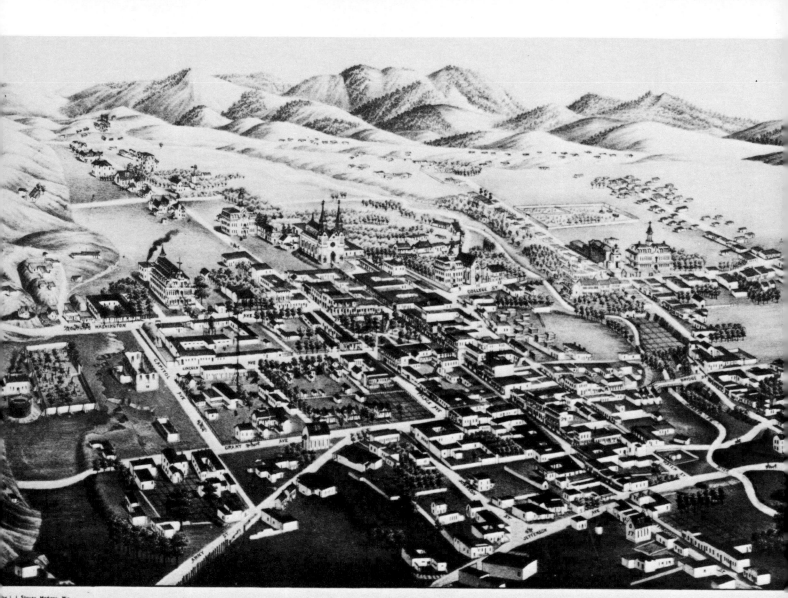

1. Palace.
2. H'd Qrs. Dist. N. M.
3. Post of Fort Marcy.
4. Government Corral.
5. First National Bank of Santa Fe.
6. Second National Bank of New Mexico.
7. Cathedral.
8. St. Vincent Hospital.
9. Academy,
10. Chapel,   Sisters of Loretto.
12. Convent,
13. St. Michaels College.
14. San Miguel Church. Erected in 1582, distroyed by
    Indians 1680, rebuilt 1710 by the Marquis de la Penuela.
15. Congregational Church.

BIRD'S EYE VIEW OF THE CITY OF

SANTA FÉ, N.M.
1882.

Copyright 1882 by J. J. Stoner, Madison, Wis.

Bird's-Eye View

This bird's-eye view of 1882 Santa Fe reveals both existing and former structures. The spires of St. Francis Cathedral were never completed; many who viewed them as foreign and discordant with Santa Fe believed this was fortunate. Note the large area occupied by military forces north of the Plaza (the old presidio grounds of the pre-Anglo-American days). The building to become the U.S. Courthouse (on Capitol Avenue in this drawing) is shown here uncompleted. It was not finished until seven years after this drawing was made. The shell of the first floor remained uncompleted for decades.

Photo courtesy of the Museum of New Mexico (negative no. 23306)

Guadalupe Church.
M. E. Church.
Presbyterian Church.
Episcopal Church.
Oldest Building in Santa-Fe.
Palace Hotel, P. Rumsey & Son.
Exchange Hotel, Reed & Bishop.
Capitol Hotel, Gray & Bailey.
Herlow's Hotel, P. F. Herlow.
Santa-Fe Planing Mill, P. Hesch.
Cracker Factory, D. L. Miller & Co.
Post Office.
Depot.
Gas Works.
Fisher Brewing Co.'s Brewery.

Lamy Group

As if frozen in a tableau, Archbishop Lamy (second from left) and some of his clerics (Bishop J. P. Machebeuf is to his immediate left) posed for the camera. They were probably in the archbishop's gardens at the time, in the latter part of Lamy's tenure in Santa Fe.

Photo courtesy of the State Records Center and Archives

53

First Capital

The first building to serve as New Mexico's capitol after the Palace of the Governors was the one seen at the extreme right in this photo. Constructed in 1885, it mysteriously burned in 1892. In the center-rear is St. Francis Cathedral. The photographer was facing north-northeast.

Courtesy of the Zimmerman Library, University of New Mexico, Ladd Collection

Ramona School

The Ramona School was founded in Santa Fe in 1885, and was divided into the Ramona School for Indian Girls and the Ramona Industrial School of the University of New Mexico (no connection to the present university). Located on College Street south of DeVargas Street, the school was funded by the United States government, the American Missionary Association, the university, and individual contributions. The famed architect Stanford White once designed a building for the school, but it was never built.

This photograph of six young students at the Ramona School for Indian Girls illustrated a November 1893 article in **Worthington's** Magazine. *Photograph courtesy of the Museum of New Mexico*

Cathedral Drawing

St. Francis Cathedral does not look like this today, although, had the money not run out, these towers would have been constructed. Instead, the three-story towers were left out, and the church today has two unidentical shorter towers. (One is topped off by stone pieces making it look much like a rook in chess, while the other is smooth on top.) William G. Ritch, in his book Aztlan, *published in 1885, jumped the gun by reproducing this drawing purporting to be the cathedral when it never did receive these finishing touches. Had it these towers, the cathedral would dominate Santa Fe even more than it already does.*

Photo courtesy of the Museum of New Mexico (negative no. 10005)

Headquarters

In 1885, when this drawing was published by the Bureau of Immigration in Santa Fe, the military complex still dominated much of Santa Fe around the Palace of the Governors. "The Fort" is the hillside Fort Marcy, which was never used. Instead, the military life centered on the area in the foreground. The "Old Spanish Government Palace" to the extreme right is the Palace of the Governors. The building to the immediate left of it is the site of today's Museum of Fine Arts.

Drawing reproduced from Illustrated New Mexico *by William G. Ritch; photo courtesy of the State Records Center and Archives, Bergere Family Collection*

Lew Wallace Building

Today, this 1887 building on the campus of St. Michael's College (El Colegio de San Miguel) is now the Lew Wallace Building, used by the state government. Drastically remodeled, it stands behind the San Miguel Chapel and across DeVargas Street from La Paloma restaurant. Like many buildings in Santa Fe, the roof has been changed from a pitched one to a flat one, and the exterior surface has been plastered to give it a "Santa Fe look."

Photo courtesy of the Christian Brothers and St. Michael's High School

West View From St. Mike's

Looking west from the St. Michael's campus on College Street one could see these small adobe dwellings and gardens in the 1880s. Much of Santa Fe at that time was composed of such housing and land use. In the background is the private school known as the University of New Mexico (now University Plaza at Garfield and Guadalupe streets).

Photo courtesy of the Christian Brothers and St. Michael's High School

Northwest View From St. Mike's

In the 1880s this was the view from the top of St. Michael's College when one looked to the northwest. Today, of course, this area of fields is filled with streets, houses, and offices.

Photo courtesy of the Christian Brothers and St. Michael's High School

North View From St. Mike's

North of the campus of St. Mike's were these buildings. To the extreme left is the unfinished St. Francis Cathedral (on which construction began in 1869) with La Parroquia extant inside it. Behind the church is the St. Vincent Sanatorium (1883-96). The tower and roof of San Miguel Chapel are at the bottom of this photo.

Photo courtesy of the Christian Brothers and St. Michael's High School

Faithway House

One of the more unusual houses in Santa Fe has long been the Cuyler Preston house, sometimes called the Faithway house because of its location on the tiny Faithway Street. Today, this Queen Anne-style house is a bed-and-breakfast establishment. It served not only as a private residence in previous years, but was also used for offices. One former resident cared for so many birds that the house was once nicknamed "the bird house." It was built in 1886.

Photo by David Grant Noble; courtesy of the Museum of New Mexico (negative no. 56839)

First Ward School

The First Ward School, located at the corner of Garcia Street (sometimes referred to in earlier documents as Caminos de los Garcias) and Canyon Road (referred to in such documents as El Camino Real), was one of the first, if not the first, public school in Santa Fe. Originally a dance hall, it was purchased for a school in 1876. It was replaced with a brick structure (still standing) in 1906.

Photo courtesy of the State Records Center and Archives

Baseball Club

The baseball club of 1888 at St. Michael's College consisted of (placement in photo unknown): J. Airheart, F. Romero, E. Abeyta, B. L. Flevy, P. E. Chavez, A. Valdez, F. Aragon, J. A. Montoya, S. Baca, and B. Briggs. Although called "college" in English, the school was for elementary and secondary boys. The institution run by the Christian Brothers did offer some post-high-school courses, however.

Photo courtesy of the Christian Brothers and St. Michael's High School

Lamy in State

In 1888 retired Archbishop Jean Baptiste Lamy lay in state in Loretto Chapel, one of several Roman Catholic institutions he caused to be built in Santa Fe in the latter part of the nineteenth century.

Photo courtesy of the State Records Center and Archives, E. Boyd Collection

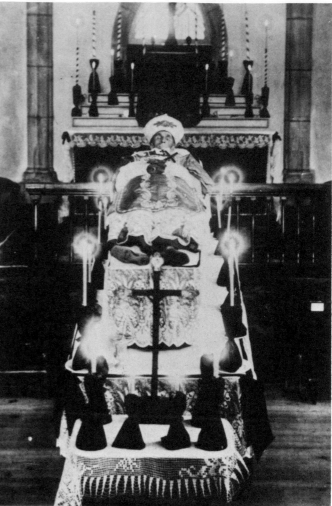

Bishop's Gardens

One of the earliest postcards of Santa Fe (made in the 1880s) showed the archbishop's gardens and residence. Today, St. Francis Cathedral School and parking areas are on this location. The residence for the archbishop has been in Albuquerque for several years.

Photo courtesy of Richard Levy and the Silver Sunbeam, Albuquerque

John B. Salpointe

John B. Salpointe (1825-98) replaced Lamy as archbishop in 1884. He arrived in the Southwest as a missionary in 1859 and was later vicar apostolic of Arizona. In 1894 he resigned as archbishop, retired to Tucson, Arizona, where he wrote the book Soldiers of the Cross *in 1898. This 1889 gravure by the Gebbie and Husson Company was made about halfway through his tenure as Lamy's successor.*

Photo courtesy of the Museum of New Mexico (negative no. 50533)

Hospital

St. Vincent's Hospital, still the sole public hospital in Santa Fe, was opened in 1865 by the Sisters of Charity, invited to Santa Fe by Archbishop Lamy. This building, originally the hospital annex and later the territory's first old folks' home, was erected in 1886, six years later than the sanatorium (to the right).

Photo courtesy of the Museum of New Mexico (negative no. 15221)

Dana B. Chase

Santa Fe from Old Ft. Marcy *is the title of this Dana B. Chase photo. Chase took many photos of places and people in nineteenth-century Santa Fe. In the middle of this photo is the Palace Hotel* (built 1880); *to the right is the Federal Building (the U.S. Courthouse); left rear can be seen the private school called the University of New Mexico at Garfield and Guadalupe streets.*

Photo courtesy of New Mexico State University, Blazer Collection, and Austin Hoover, NMSU Archivist

Reredos

The stone reredos *that had been carved for the military's chapel on the Plaza, La Castrense, was moved in 1859 (when La Castrense was sold) to the sanctuary of La Parroquia, and was later kept behind the altar of the cathedral until Cristo Rey Church was opened in 1940. The* reredos *was carved by artisans from Mexico who were brought to Santa Fe for that purpose by Governor Antonio Marín del Valle. This Charles F. Lummis photo, circa 1890, shows the* reredos *in its place behind the sanctuary of the cathedral.*

Photo courtesy of the Museum of New Mexico (negative no. 10023)

Plaza Still

A photographer froze action on the Plaza circa 1887 in a shot of this always-active part of Santa Fe. The Plaza has long been a favorite spot for teenagers to see—if not talk to—the opposite sex. Young men and women of past generations would "promenade" around the square, eyeing each other, and thoroughly enjoying themselves.

Photo courtesy of the Museum of New Mexico (negative no. 11299)

College Street

The influence of Archbishop Jean Baptiste Lamy is evident in this Santa Fe Railway photo, circa 1890, which shows, in front, part of the campus of Loretto Academy, and, at the far right, a portion of the St. Michael's College campus. Education, health, and, of course, religion were concerns of the strong-willed cleric.

Photo courtesy of the State Records Center and Archives

Harper's Page

These 1890 sketches of Santa Fe must have intrigued the readers who had never been "out West." The drawing in the bottom right, "the college," is St. Michael's College. It was called "El Colegio" because many courses were offered there that were beyond the high school level. In 1874 the territorial legislature authorized St. Michael's to confer degrees, and in 1893, it was allowed to grant its graduates teaching certificates.

Photo courtesy of the Museum of New Mexico (negative no. 105863)

Catron Block

The Catron Block, the oldest building on the Plaza (outside the Palace of the Governors, of course) was commissioned by Thomas B. Catron, local politician, lawyer, and businessman. In the Weekly New Mexico Review of September 27, 1888, Catron discussed with the architect, a man named Brigham, plans for the Catron Block: "It is more than likely that a superb brick business block with frontage on the Plaza and Palace Avenue will be erected as quickly as men and money can do it, and it is also probably thta the upper story of the structure be fitted as an opera house."

The building was erected by the firm of Palladino and Berardinelli (made up of two of the Italian families that came to Santa Fe to complete work on the cathedral and remained to construct many fine buildings in the town). Today the upper story is still occupied by the same law firm that Catron founded. (Two of his grandsons are partners.)

The building is often referred to as the Blatt Building because of the Blatt family interests in stores that have occupied the corner location (now the site of the Guarantee Store). A portal was added

years ago to bring the building into line with the others on the Plaza; the exterior stone below that portal was plastered over to make it look more "Santa Fe." However, above the portal one can still see the original stonework of a more Eastern appearance, making this building very representative of the changes in architectural fashion.

Catron held many offices. He was U.S. attorney for New Mexico, mayor of Santa Fe (1906-08), and U.S. senator from the state in 1912. He was also one of the members of the Constitutional Convention that met in Santa Fe in 1910 to prepare for statehood. Catron was the leader of the Santa Fe Ring, a group of politicians, attorneys, businessmen, and large ranchers that virtually controlled the political and economic life of New Mexico during territorial days.

Photo courtesy of T. B. Catron III

St. Vincent's

To the right is the original building used for St. Vincent's Hospital. When first built in 1853 by Carlos Brun, a seminarian, it was one story and originally used as the episcopal residence. Lamy gave the building to the newly arrived Sisters of Charity for their hospital in 1865. After they took over the building, the second story and the porches were added. To the left is Seton Hall, built in 1882 as a convent and nurses' residence. It too was later used as a hospital. The back of St. Francis Cathedral is at the upper right.

Photo courtesy of the State Records Center and Archives; original photo in archives of Sisters of Charity, Mount St. Joseph, Ohio

Magoffin View

These two women were caught by someone's camera in July 1891. The photographer was at the front door of the Magoffin house library across the street. In the background is the county courthouse that burned mysteriously in 1907. Today, the Coronado Building is on this site.

Photo courtesy of the Museum of New Mexico (negative no. 10018)

Corral

With the horse or other animal used for the conveyance of people and freight during the nineteenth century, a natural offshoot in communities like Santa Fe would be corrals for the animals, such as this one, the Dodson and Bears Transfer Corral. Note the main building of St. Michael's College in the distance.

Photo by Ben Wittick; courtesy of the Museum of New Mexico, School of American Research Collections in the Museum of New Mexico (negative no. 15826)

First Capitol

The first capitol burned in 1892, six years after it was built. The cause of this fire was never determined, but it is believed to have been arson.

Photo courtesy of the Museum of New Mexico (negative no. 16710)

State Pen

The state penitentiary, now miles outside the city limits, was at one time located at what is now the intersections of St. Francis Drive, Cordova Road, and Pen Road. This circa 1890 photo shows the prisoners in traditional striped prison clothing constructing one of the prison buildings. A popular story says that Santa Fe, given the choice of the state penitentiary or the new state university, chose the former since it provided more jobs. Albuquerque became the home of the University of New Mexico.

Photo courtesy of the Museum of New Mexico (negative no. 15208)

Ben Wittick

Unlike most Americans of the nineteenth century, Ben Wittick was quite relaxed before a camera. He should have *been. He took many important photographs of Santa Fe people and places during this period. This stereoscopic* *photo shows him in a playful mood.*

Photo courtesy of the Museum of New Mexico (negative no. 55722)

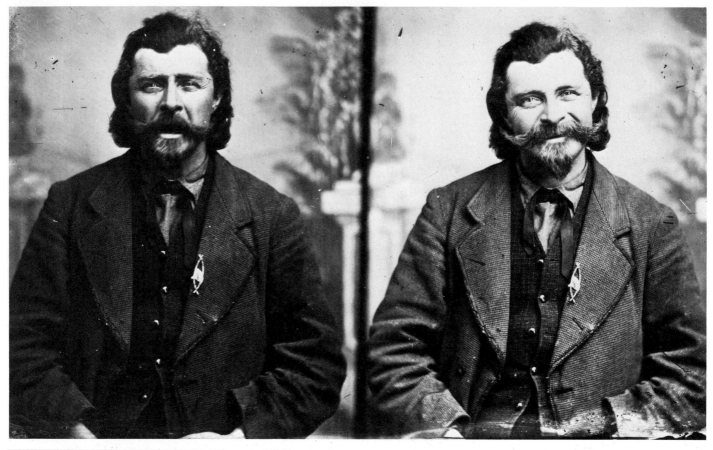

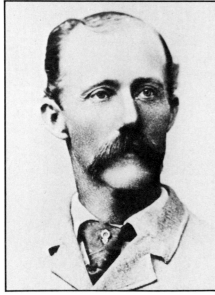

A. M. Bergere

Alfred Maurice Bergere moved to Santa Fe around the turn of the century when he became the district court clerk of the first judicial district. He had been involved in cattle, insurance, and business in Valencia County. Bergere and his wife Eloisa Luna de Otero Bergere moved into the house at 135 Grant Avenue that had been assigned by the government to her brother, Solomon Luna.

The house has been built in the early 1870s as an officer's quarters on the Fort Marcy Military Reservation (abandoned in 1894). Bergere added a second story. (Daughter Consuelo Bergere Mendenhall recalls that, in the first years of occupancy, she and her sisters would bump their heads on the low ceiling of the original house.) Bergere also built stables and tennis courts, and planted trees. Only the trees remain. The house stands between the Safeway store and the former Bataan school building on Grant Avenue.

Photo courtesy of the Museum of New Mexico (negative no. 47692)

Eloisa Luna

Eloisa Luna de Otero Bergere raised her children in luxury in Santa Fe. She was described by historian-politician Ralph Emerson Twitchell as "the most beautiful woman in New Mexico." She was born in Los Lunas (founded by her ancestors). Eloisa Luna went by covered wagon to St. Louis to attend Catholic school. Her first husband, Manuel B. Otero, had attended Heidelberg University in Germany. Their marriage in 1879 began with a gondola trip down the Rio Grande (accompanied by guitarists). Three years after his death in a shoot-out over a land dispute she married A. M. Bergere.

Daughter Consuelo remembers being taken to the Plaza at certain times of the week by the family's live-in nanny to listen to band concerts. One of Mrs. Bergere's children by her first marriage

was Adelina Otero-Warren, a well-known author.

Photo courtesy of the Museum of New Mexico (negative no. 22929)

Capitol columns

Shortly before the "new" state capitol was completed in 1900, these columns and bases rested outside the state prison awaiting delivery to the capitol site.

Barely more than fifty years later, they would be removed because the capitol was being renovated to make it look more "Santa Fe."

Photo courtesy of the State Records Center and Archives, Adella Collier collection

Otero Residence

First used as the commanding officer's quarters for Fort Marcy, this house later became the Governor Miguel Otero residence. Later, it was the Santa Fe Club. In 1982 the First Interstate Bank began construction of new facilities on this and neighboring lots, and a hasty archaeological dig resulted in the uncovering of artifacts of the Spanish and territorial eras.

Photo courtesy of the Museum of New Mexico (negative no. 1695)

Palace

For many decades, this is what the Palace looked like. It was not until 1912-13 that Jesse Nusbaum was given the task of removing the Victorian look and returning the building to a Spanish-Pueblo style.

Photo courtesy of the State Records Center and Archives, Historic Santa Fe Foundation Collection

Fort Marcy

Fort Marcy, that military complex that covered much of the present-day commercial section of downtown Santa Fe north of the Palace of the Governors, contained a number of officers' houses such as this one on Grant Avenue. Two are still in existence today, the Bergere house at 135 Grant Avenue, and the Hewett house, just north of the Museum of Fine Arts at 116 Lincoln Avenue. There were originally six adobe houses constructed for the use of the officers at the fort.

Photo courtesy of the State Records Center and Archives, Sylvia Loomis Collection

Adolph Bandelier

Adolph Bandelier, Swiss-born archaeologist and writer, lived in Santa Fe (he rented a house at 352 East DeVargas Street) and did much of his work in this part of the world. An hour's drive from Santa Fe is Bandelier National Monument, which contains Native American dwellings from early in this millenium that were explored by him.

Photo by Edouard Melly; courtesy of the Museum of New Mexico (negative no. 7052)

Hayt-Wientge House

This picture perhaps more than any other shows the contrast to two Santa Fes developing in the latter part of the 1800s. In the background is the Hayt-Wientge house, still a part of the Santa Fe "skyline," *and a model of the Victorian-era architecture that was imported into Santa Fe during this period. In front is an adobe house like those present in the town from the beginning and which still*

remain as the symbol of architecture for the capital city. In fact, some buildings looking much like the Hayt-Wientge house were covered over in the Spanish-Pueblo adobe style when the twentieth-century Santa Fe style took hold. A great diversity in architectural styles was lost in the process.

The Hayt-Wientge house was built in 1882 (the same year as the Staab house) by Walter V. Hayt, a prominent Santa Fe merchant who operated a store on the main business thoroughfare, San Francisco Street. This and the Hesch house on Read Street are the only two houses remaining that have mansard roofs. In 1888 Hayt sold this house to Mrs. Christina F. Wientge, wife of Frederick W. Wientge, a jeweler whose silver-turquoise work was exhibited at the 1893 Columbia Exposition in Chicago. He built a small adobe room just north of the mansion for use as a jewelry shop. The house was occupied by the Wientge family until 1972.

Photo by Dana Chase; courtesy of the Museum of New Mexico (negative no. 89281)

Garden Party

Ben Wittick captured these Santa Feans and travelers in a "summer garden" atmosphere in a now-unknown location in the late 1800s. Stereoscopic views of Santa Fe must have been popular around the United States and helped attract visitors to this small but very cosmopolitan territorial capital.

Photo courtesy of the Museum of New Mexico (negative no. 15814)

Kaune's

Still a familiar name to Santa Feans, Kaune's first existed on the south side of the Plaza. This site is near the present Häagen-Dazs ice cream parlor. Henry Spencer Kaune was born in Illinois; he came to Santa Fe around 1880 and established this store. The mayor's office was upstairs and Charles Haspelmath Boot and Shoes "leather and fittings" was to the east. (He was later bought out by John Pflueger.) Kaune's moved to the Old Santa Fe Trail location in 1950, and the Washington Avenue store opened in 1956.

Photo courtesy of Julie Kaune

Isabel Cabeza de Vaca

Isabel Cabeza de Vaca, wife of Major José D. Sena, builder of Sena Plaza, posed for the camera at Mrs. Albright's Art Parlors, Albuquerque, in the latter part of the nineteenth century. Their marriage brought together two prominent Spanish families.

Photo courtesy of Amalia Sena Sanchez

Star Restaurant

The Star Restaurant occupied the site of the current Plaza Cafe on the west side of the Plaza. The number of businesses that have existed on the Plaza since its inception will never be known, but it must be in the hundreds.

Photo courtesy of the Museum of New Mexico (negative no. 35868)

José Sena

José D. Sena served as a major in the Civil War on the Union side. He inherited the property known as the Sena Plaza through his mother, Maria del Rosario Alaríd. It had originally been part of a grant from Don Diego deVargas to a Captain Arias de Quiros. Sena expanded the property from a small house and placita ("little plaza") to a much larger house containing thirty-three rooms. Today, Sena Plaza, after undergoing some architectural changes by William Penhallow Henderson, the architect-painter who was active in the local artists' community in the early twentieth century, is home to many businesses and officer.

Photo by Mrs. Albright's Art Parlors, Albuquerque; courtesy of Amalia Sena Sanchez

Delgado Children

Elena Delgado and José Gonzales posed for the photographer around 1895. José sported a "summer haircut," a custom still practiced occasionally in Santa Fe. Elena was José's aunt, despite their closeness in age, a situation not uncommon in families with many children in each generation.

Photo courtesy of Anita Gonzales Thomas

75

Otero Inauguration

Miguel A. Otero, the only Hispanic governor during the territorial period (Donanciano Vigil was acting governor after the assassination of Governor Charles Bent in 1847), was inaugurated on June 14, 1897, the date of this photo. Hundreds gathered in front of the Palace (no longer used for the governor's offices) to witness his inauguration. Otero was appointed governor by President McKinley, and later reappointed by President Theodore Roosevelt, ending his term of office in 1906.

Photo by P. E. Harroun; courtesy of the Museum of New Mexico (negative no. 14090)

Candelario

Jesús "J. C." Candelario, "the Curio Man," was an important figure in the tourist-oriented market for Santa Fe in the nineteenth and twentieth centuries. Candelario curios were marketed to all who came to town, and anyone looking for something to take back home to relatives in the East only had to visit his curio shop on West San Francisco Street to find something of interest. Candelario was well known enough in his own right to appear on a postcard sold in his shop.

Photo courtesy of John S. Candelario

San Miguel Interior

San Miguel Chapel as it looked in 1898 was not that different from what it looks like today. Some of the religious figures and art work seen here remain in the chapel; the major changes to the chapel have taken place to the exterior.

Photo attributed to Harry C. Yontz; courtesy of Gladys Gilmour

New Mexican Close-Up

Today, most newspapers, including Santa Fe's New Mexican and Santa Fe Reporter, avail themselves of computer technology, but things were a little slower in 1899, when these employees posed for this photo. At the turn of the century, the New Mexican staff included (left to right): Miss Swope, Henry Pacheco, an unidentified woman, Paul A. F. Walter, Colonel Max Frost, and Elmer Marsh.

Photo courtesy of the Museum of New Mexico (negative no. 15275)

Roque Lovato House

The Roque Lovato house, located across the street from the present Scottish Rite Temple at Paseo de Peralta and Bishop's Lodge Road, is shown here as it looked for much of its life before being rehabilitated in the twentieth century. It became the home of Sylvanus G. Morley, the archaeologist, who was one of the Santa Feans interested in reestablishing a Santa Fe style in the early 1900s. (He also served as director of the Museum of New Mexico.)

The building stands in front of the now-extinct La Garita, an old Spanish-era watchtower that was built circa 1805-08 on top of prehistoric and early historic Indian house mounds. La Garita was a favorite Sunday picnic ground for Santa Feans equipped with picks and shovels for pot-hunting.

Photo courtesy of the Museum of New Mexico (negative no. 10543)

Placita

This quiet, almost pastoral scene was taken inside a placita in Santa Fe (possibly Prince Plaza) sometime in the latter part of the nineteenth century. Such courtyards were not uncommon and served utilitarian functions as well as gathering places for the families who lived there.

Photo courtesy of the Zimmerman Library, University of New Mexico, Horatio Ladd Collection

Postcard

City fathers probably approved of the slogan "Oldest City in the U.S." for Santa Fe, which was already catching the more adventuresome tourists' eyes in the late nineteenth century. This postcard, a rare one, was produced by Santa Fe merchant Charles Haspelmath (owner of the shoe store), and this particular copy carried the name "John Pflueger" at the top, stamped on by the shoe store merchant who no doubt gave or sold these to his customers. Although Pflueger did not open his store until 1910, this card was made in the 1890s and was one of a series of cards featuring Santa Fe made in that decade.

Photo courtesy of Richard Levy and the Silver Sunbeam, Albuquerque

Chapter Six
1900-1912:

From Territory To Statehood

The period in question, 1900-12, was one of transition. Not only was Santa Fe going through the first dozen years of a new century, it was in the process of changing from the capital of a territory to one of a state.

Agitation for statehood began almost from the moment Brigadier-General Stephen Watts Kearny arrived to seize the area for the United States in 1846. Serious attempts were first made in 1850, and throughout the remainder of the nineteenth century, to bring New Mexico into the U.S. as a full-fledged state. Joint statehood for Arizona and New Mexico was attempted in 1906, but Arizonians rejected the proposal. In 1910 the U.S. Congress passed an enabling act which resulted in a constitutional convention held in Santa Fe the same year. The outcome was a constitution that was ratified by the voters of New Mexico in January 1911. On January 6, 1912, President William Howard Taft signed a bill that admitted New Mexico as the forty-seventh state.

The motor car made its appearance in Santa Fe during this period, but it was not yet a strong influence in the town. By statehood, it was more commonplace, but it was still out of reach for the average Santa Fean.

Public school education had begun in the late 1800s, but great strides were made during the early years of the twentieth century to educate many young Santa Feans. Parochial schools, particularly Roman Catholic ones, were also busy with the task of educating youth, and a few Indian boarding schools catered to students from a wide geographic area.

No records exist to tell us how many tourists came to Santa Fe during this twelve-year period, but we do know that more and more postcards were produced (and purchased and mailed to everyone back home), and such establishments as Jesús (J. C.) Candelario's Curio Store abounded in goods sought by the wide-eyed "dudes" from the East Coast states.

Santa Fe was on its way to becoming a mecca for travelers seeking something different.

Sena as Washington

José D. Sena portrayed a little George Washington in Mrs. Fletcher's kindergarten class (in the present Bishop Building on West Palace Avenue), and Jane Abott, daughter of a judge, played his wife Martha.

Photo courtesy of Amalia Sena Sanchez

Wedding Party

All the rooms of the Palace Hotel were taken over for the wedding party of Charles Abreu and Carmen Sena on Washington's Birthday, 1900. The two women in dark clothing on the left are unidentified guests; the rest of the party consisted of, left to right: Vito Abreu, sister of the groom; Mary Sena, sister of the bride; the groom; the bride; Sophie Abreu, sister of the groom; Adelina Otero, a relative of the Sena family. The little girl on the left is May Bergere, and the one on the right is Amalia Sena (now Mrs. Amalia Sanchez). The bride's father built Sena Plaza.

Photo courtesy of Amalia Sena Sanchez

Exchange Hotel

The Exchange Hotel, on the site of the present LaFonda, included the Kinsell Livestock Company Meat Market on the premises, shown in this 1900-05 photo. Note the adobe bricks at the bottom right of the building that show through the exterior plaster covering.

Photo courtesy of the Museum of New Mexico (negative no. 105576)

Puck

New Mexico tried and tried to become a state, and finally succeeded in 1912. This cover of Puck shows "New Mexico" in 1901 begging to be given the Cloak of Statehood.

Photo courtesy of the Museum of New Mexico

VOL. L. No. 1294.   PUCK BUILDING, New York, December 18th, 1901.   PRICE TEN CENTS.
Copyright, 1901, by Keppler & Schwarzmann.

Entered at N. Y. P. O. as Second-class Mail Matter.

Fiske

Josie (Mrs. E. A.) Fiske shielded her eyes from the sun on a bright afternoon sometime between 1900 and 1905 while she watched these two young girls pose on burros. On the left was Genevieve Harrison, and on the right was Helen Harrison. Santa Fe receives relatively little precipitation compared to much of the United States; the portales ("porches") on either side of the street served more to protect the pedestrian from the intense afternoon sun. If one follows San Francisco Street, where this photo was taken, to the end one comes to St. Francis Cathedral, a landmark as familiar today as it was at the turn of the century.

Photo by C. G. Kaadt; courtesy of the Museum of New Mexico (negative no. 11341)

CANDELARIO'S

Do you know Old Candelario's
   Indian relics and curios?
Anyone can show you the way
   In the ancient town of Santa Fé
To Candelario's.

In the shop beneath the old ox cart
   All the products of Indian art
Has Candelario.
   Bows and baskets and pottery
Beaten silver and filigree—
   Every old kind of trumpery
Has Candelario.

For an Indian blanket you want to go
   To Candelario.
He has zerapes and Chimayos,
   Old bayettas and Navajos—
There are all the kinds that anyone knows
   At Candelario's.

Should it be that you want a gem,
   Candelario has them.
Sapphires, garnets, and turquois blue,
   Amethysts. rubies and opals. too,
As good as you want he can furnish you
   Can Candelario.

In the ancient town of Santa Fé
   Is Candelario.
Anyone can show you the way
   To Candelario.
For anything you want to know—
   For any kind of a curio—
Go to CANDELARIO
            J. S. CANDELARIO.

Candelario's Cart

The cart depicted on this postcard was the trademark of the Candelario shop for many decades. It rested on the roof and drew visitors to the premises where they would find an enormous assortment of things to marvel over—and buy. Candelario's was truly the place to go "for any kind of a curio."

Photo courtesy of John S. Candelario

Old Curio Store

The Old Curio Store of Jesús "J. C." Candelario on West San Francisco Street was a popular place for tourists in the late nineteenth and twentieth centuries. Jesús is seen here at the left, with his daughter on the right. No doubt the merchandise seen in this photo can be found in attics all over the United States today.

Photo courtesy of John S. Candelario

DeForest and May

DeForest Dodge Lord, Sr., and Maria "May" Bernadette Bergere posed very solemnly for the photographer in the early years of this century. DeForest grew up to be a dentist as was his father. May married John Kenny; she served with the National Youth Administration (NYA) and was clerk of the Santa Fe draft board for many years. DeForest's mother, Marietta Dodge Phelps, later married Aloysius B. Renehan, a criminal lawyer who was a member of the Santa Fe Ring. May's parents were A. M. and Eloisa Bergere, shown earlier in the book.
Photo courtesy of David Lord

Gold's

Jake Gold, for some time a partner of Jesús Candelario, had his own Old Curiosity Shop on Burro Alley for many years. It was advertised as having begun in 1862. This turn-of-the-century photo shows the old adobe building with Indian-made blankets on some of the posts, put there to entice out-of-town customers.
Photo courtesy of David Lord

Horno

The horno *("oven") is used on the Indian pueblos today to bake fine bread, eaten by resident and tourist alike, but the ones in use in this Santa Fe home early in this century were for family cooking. Homes such as this one were purchased later in the century, given a "finished" look, modernized inside, and now bring a price that earlier inhabitants would have found unbelievable.*

Photo courtesy of the Museum of New Mexico (negative no. 11165). Photo by C. G. Kaadt

Vierra

Carlos Vierra, a Californian descended from Portuguese settlers of the Azores, moved to Santa Fe in 1904. Vierra painted murals of pre-Columbian cities of the Yucatan in the New Mexico building at the Panama-San Diego Exposition; the building, named the Cathedral of the Desert, was based on old Southwestern buildings, including the church at Acoma Pueblo, west of Albuquerque. These murals are still in the Hall of Man in Balboa Park in San Diego.

Vierra also completed the Beauregard murals in the St. Francis Auditorium of the Museum of Fine Arts after the original artist died. These were painted between 1912 and 1915. The head of Christopher Columbus in those murals is a Vierra self-portrait. He is shown here painting a Mayan courtyard scene while employed by the School of American Archaeology, the predecessor of today's School of American Research.

Photo courtesy of the State Records Center and Archives, Historic Santa Fe Foundation Collection

1903 Baseball Team

Looking like something out of "Our Gang," the St. Michael's College baseball team of 1903 posed in front of the dormitory. Back row, left to right, are: Alfredo Valdez and Jerry Kelly; middle row, left to right, Gilbert Mirobel, Juan Miera, A. Alarid, Max Tafoya, and Ferederico Soto; and seated, left to right, Jose R. Martinez, Severo G. Soto, and Frank Luna. A note on the old photo said, "Played together for 3 years—very good team."

Photo courtesy of College of Santa Fe and the Christian Brothers

Nazario Gonzales

Nazario Gonzales stood stiffly in front of the camera for his first communion picture sometime between 1905 and 1910. It was customary to come into the church for one's first communion holding a candle decorated with cloth or silk flowers purchased from a shop like Mugler's Millinery (that used to be on the Plaza across from LaFonda). The photographer of this particular picture may have been Nicholas Brown, who lived for some time with the Delgado family on the Plaza. Nazario Gonzales was a relative of the Delgado family.

Photo courtesy of Anita Gonzales Thomas

Butcher Shop

On the south side of Water Street near its intersection with Sandoval Street was the location of this butcher shop around 1905-10. Hijinio Pacheco stood in the middle and Ramon Pacheco on the left. The man on the left is identified only as Hilario. This shop can quickly be contrasted to a meat market of today.

Photo courtesy of the Museum of New Mexico (negative no. 10663)

HON. MIGUEL A. OTERO
SANTA FE

Otero Cartoon

The Las Vegas Optic, one of the state's oldest newspapers, showed Governor Miguel Otero in this pose when he was ready to leave the governorship in 1906, having served the longest of any of the territorial governors.

Photo courtesy of the Museum of New Mexico (negative no. 7748)

First Ward School

Carlos Digneo built the First Ward School in 1906. This is now the Linda Durham Gallery on Canyon Road at Garcia Street. The Digneo family came to Santa Fe, along with the Palladino and Berardinelli families, to finish the work on St. Francis Cathedral. They remained to build other fine structures.

Photo courtesy of the State Records Center and Archives

Ralph Emerson Twitchell

Ralph Emerson Twitchell (1859-1925) left his stamp on Santa Fe through his writings (he published several books on the town), his legal career with the Santa Fe Railroad, and his involvement in local politics (he was mayor 1893-94).

Photo courtesy of the Museum of New Mexico (negative no. 13372)

St. Francis Cathedral

St. Francis Cathedral around 1907 was an ornate structure that served then, as it does today, as the primary Roman Catholic church in the Archdiocese of Santa Fe. At that time, the building was part of a large church complex that included St. Vincent's Sanatorium, St. Vincent's Hospital, and St. Vincent's Orphanage, all administered by the Sisters of Charity.

Photo by R. A. Fiske; courtesy of the Museum of New Mexico (negative no. 10020)

Courthouse Ruins

A 1907 fire destroyed the Santa Fe County Courthouse, a large brick structure at East Palace Avenue and Otero Street. Local residents enjoyed the many shows that were available in the courthouse on Sunday afternoons during the 1890s and the first few years of this century.

Photo by Anna L. Hase; courtesy of the Museum of New Mexico (negative no. 105580)

State Pen

The state penitentiary was first located near the present Coronado Shopping Center. The only vestiges of the original are the names Pen Road and Pen Road Shopping Center. Today, the penitentiary is located a few miles south of Santa Fe; it attracted world attention because of a bloody riot in 1980.

Photo by Jesse Nusbaum; courtesy of Richard Levy and the Silver Sunbeam, Albuquerque

Bynner Property

What is now known as the Witter Bynner house stands on this property and incorporates most of the houses seen here. Bynner eventually purchased the front two houses and joined them, completing a renovation begun by artist Andrew Dasburg. An old well stands next to the house on the right. The house on the left was the home of artist Louise Crow and also of Paul Burlin; the one on the right was occupied first by Dasburg, then by Bynner. The house behind the Crow-Burlin house belonged to Ben Muniz, a local landlord and at one time editor of the Spanish-language edition of the New Mexican. This photo was taken circa 1907-09. The Bynner house stands at the corner of Buena Vista Street and Old Santa Fe Trail.

Photo by Ferneley Wiley; courtesy of Gladys Gilmour

San Miguel

San Miguel Chapel looked like this when tourists roamed the town in 1909. The building at the right was the boys' dormitory; it is now the Lamy Building, a state government office building.

Photo courtesy of the Museum of New Mexico (negative no. 48338)

College Street

This view, taken circa 1907-10, shows College Street, looking north toward town. Today, this is once again the Old Santa Fe Trail near the intersection of Buena Vista Street, which intersects College at the end of the fence on the left. The cattle of José Sena, son of the builder of Sena Plaza, are on their way to a mesa to graze. This street looked much like this until it was paved in the 1920s. The Old Santa Fe Trail was also known as "the road to Independence," and is so marked on some maps.

Photo by Ferneley Wiley; courtesy of Gladys Gilmour

The Willows

The Willows, the residence of Aloysius B. Renehan (1869-1928), local criminal lawyer, and his wife, Marietta Dodge Phelps Lord Renehan, looked like this early in this century. The house was originally a brewery. Today, it survives—with its top story missing—on East Palace Avenue, an address for many of the town's wealthy, influential citizens of decades ago. Mr. Renehan was a member of the Santa Fe Ring, a group of local politicians and others who held control of much of the political and economic affairs of the territory. After his death, Mrs. Renehan lived as a recluse until her own death in 1964.

Photo courtesy of David Lord

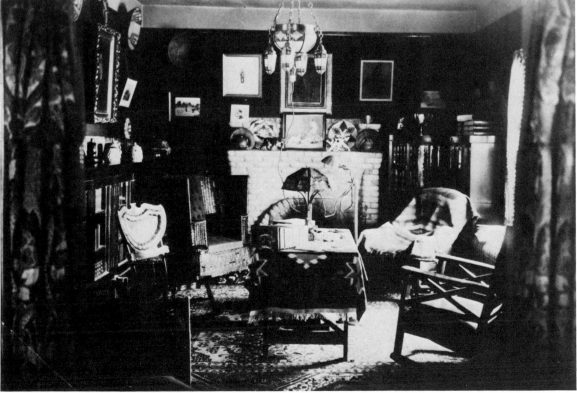

Digneo House

The house on the right would be smack in the middle of the Paseo de Peralta if it were standing today. At that time, it was the John Digneo house and stood on the northeast corner of College and Manhattan streets. College was renamed Old Santa Fe Trail, and much of Manhattan disappeared when the Paseo de Peralta was constructed. Down on the left is the Manderfield home, near the site of today's Bull Ring restaurant. Through the pillars of the Digneo house one can see a part of St. Michael's College (now the Lamy Building). Just to the south of the Digneo house is now the shopping center containing Fraser Pharmacy and Kaune's grocery store. Ferneley Wiley, the photographer, was standing in the intersection of Manhattan and College streets when he took this photo, circa 1908-09.

Other Digneo family homes still remain. The Digneo-Moore house is at 1233 Paseo de Peralta, and next door, at 1231, is the Digneo-Valdes house. The latter address was once 132 East *Manhattan Avenue. That house was constructed in 1911. A Digneo house at 512 Webber has been stuccoed since it was built.*

Photo courtesy of Gladys Gilmour

Bishop Building

What was once the site of the Fort Marcy Military Reservation bakery is now the Bishop Building on West Palace Avenue. The bakery was built soon after Kearny's arrival in 1846. Later, this building was constructed and was used as a public-school kindergarten with a Mrs. Fletcher as teacher (1899-1907). It was then rented to a Mrs. Campbell for a steam laundry in 1908.

Paul A. F. Walter bought this structure in 1909 for the New Mexican. The newspaper inhabited this building, under different ownership, until early 1942, when C. A. Bishop purchased and remodeled it. When the top-secret Manhattan Project began at nearby Los Alamos during World War II, the military assigned to the project first showed up at this building to be given instructions and directions before reporting to "the Hill" (Los Alamos).

Photo courtesy of the State Records Center and Archives

Memorial Visit

Looking like a social gathering, this is in reality a Memorial Day visit to the National Cemetery in 1909 by a group of young Santa Fe women. The National Cemetery was established in Santa Fe in 1875 and contains graves of such prominent people as Governor Charles Bent, Major General Patrick J. Hurley, and Oliver LaFarge. The initial plot of land had belonged to Roman Catholic Diocese of Santa Fe; Archbishop Lamy donated the land to the federal government.

Governor Bent, who was killed in 1847, was reinterred from the Masonic cemetery in Santa Fe to this one in 1895.

His stone reads: "He was a man of kind and gentle manners; of true benevolence of heart; of untarnished probity and lofty carriage, he laid down his life to save those dearer to him than life itself." Bent, who was killed by Mexican nationalists and Indians unhappy with the conquest of the Anglo-Americans, had a grandfather who also had had something to do with Indians: He had been a member of the Boston Tea Party. Veterans of many wars are buried in this cemetery, including Confederates who were killed in New Mexico.

Photo courtesy of the Museum of New Mexico (negative no. 5762)

Constitutional Convention

Santa Fe was the seat of a bustling, exciting convention in 1910 when the constitution for the upcoming state of New Mexico was drawn up. These delegates representing Santa Fe County were, left to right, front row: B. F. Pankey, T. B. Catron, and George W. Prichard. Top row, left to right, Victor Ortega and José D. Sena.

Photo courtesy of the Museum of New Mexico (negative no. 105864); from New Mexico Constitutional Convention Book 1910, *published by C. S. Peterson*

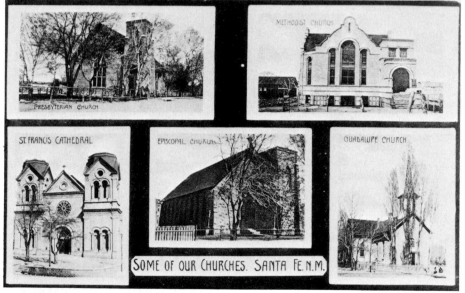

Postcard Churches

This German-made postcard was printed sometime before 1910. All these churches are found in Santa Fe today, except for the Methodist one, which was located just south of the present DeVargas Hotel on what is now a vacant lot. The Guadalupe and Presbyterian churches today have altered appearances.

Photo courtesy of Richard Levy and the Silver Sunbeam, Albuquerque

Pflueger Trip

Back to the old country for a visit went the Pflueger family in 1910, four years before their country of origin, Germany, became one of the belligerents in the "Great War." Here, Hansel and his parents, John and Louise Pflueger, posed for a ship photographer in the relatively calm years before the war. Many of the merchant families in Santa Fe had German origins.

Photo courtesy of Hansel Pflueger

Plaza Parade

Some unspecified celebration (perhaps the Fourth of July) caused this parade to make its way through the Plaza, still the favorite place to stage any colorful celebration in Santa Fe. The buildings on the left are on the south side of the Plaza.

Photo by Henry Dendahl; courtesy of the Museum of New Mexico (negative no. 15262)

Sanatorium

Snow lay on the ground in the winter of 1911 in Santa Fe as construction proceeded on the new St. Vincent Sanatorium (the spelling the Sisters of Charity always used, to designate the treatment of tuberculosis rather than the general "sanitarium"). This building was remodeled in 1954, the year the new St. Vincent's Hospital opened, and was renamed Marian Hall, becoming a convent *(the first two floors) and a residence for nurses (third floor). In 1977 the hospital complex was closed and another hospital, still called St. Vincent's, opened on St. Michael's Drive. The Sisters relinquished control of St. Vincent's in 1973.*

Photo by Jesse Nusbaum; courtesy of the Museum of New Mexico (negative no. 61372)

Governor Mills

Governor William J. Mills (left), the last territorial governor of New Mexico, sat in his carriage in front of the Palace Hotel on his way to his own inaugural in 1910. Two years later, New Mexico became the forty-seventh state of the United States, reaching a goal many New Mexicans had sought for more than sixty years, almost since the arrival of Kearny in 1846.

Photo by Theodore Asplund; courtesy of the Museum of New Mexico (negative no. 8113)

Morley House

The archaeologist Sylvanus G. Morley built this house for his mother-in-law, Frances Rhoads, directly behind his own house (see page 78). Unlike the Morley house, this one faced Bishop's Lodge Road. In the background can be seen the remains of La Garita, the Spanish-era watchtower. Morley, a strong proponent of Santa Fe style, followed that mode of architecture when building the Rhoads house.

Photo by T. Harmon Parkhurst; courtesy of the Museum of New Mexico (negative no. 14018)

Sunmount

Sunmount Sanitarium began as a tent city in 1903 under the direction of Dr. Frank Mera to aid the many "lungers" who were coming to Santa Fe to seek aid for their various ailments, principally tuberculosis. It was thought that the altitude and the relatively humidity-free air would improve their conditions, if not cure them. Santa Fe benefited greatly by this influx of people and gained such luminaries as the architect John Gaw Meem and the writer Witter Bynner who came to Santa Fe for health reasons—and who stayed to make their marks on the town.

Sunmount, named after a nearby hill, soon had more permanent buildings, and catered to hundreds of displaced Easterners. Sunmount patients are shown here with one of the sanitarium's nurses.

Sunmount later became a hotel, the Santa Fe Inn. Today, the Immaculate Heart of Mary Seminary, designed by John Gaw Meem, occupies the site. One of the seminary buildings was originally a sanitarium building.

Photo courtesy of the State Records Center and Archives, John Gaw Meem Collection

St. Catherine's

St. Catherine Industrial Indian School, shown here in one of the many 1912 photos of Santa Fe by Jesse Nusbaum, is now St. Catherine Indian School, a coed boarding/day school. The main building (with the bell tower) was constructed in 1886-87, and the school opened under the direction of the Benedictines in the fall of 1887, after its dedication by Archbishop Salpointe, with retired Archbishop Lamy in attendance.

After the departure of the Benedictines, the school was run by the Sisters of Loretto, who were also in charge of the Loretto Academy for Girls; upon their leaving the school, a lay group ran it for one year. The school was closed for the 1893-94 session, then reopened by a brand-new order, the Sisters of the Blessed Sacrament, which continues to run the school today. The founder of the S. B. S. was Mother Katharine who, as laywoman Kate Drexel of Philadelphia, financed the building of the immense

structure seen here, much as she financed the building of schools for blacks and Indians around the country. She had no idea in 1887 that she would found an order, much less that it would be in charge of this school.

Photo courtesy of the Museum of New Mexico (negative no. 61553)

Plaza Fourth

Fourth of July on the Plaza on an unspecified year found this crowd enjoying the shade of the many tall trees that filled the square.

Photo courtesy of the Museum of New Mexico (negative no. 11278)

Woman's Board of Trade

The Woman's Board of Trade building, the present main branch of the public library on Washington Avenue, is shown here in 1912. It was remodeled in 1933-34 by John Gaw Meem in territorial style, one more building in downtown Santa Fe to lose its original character and become part of Santa Fe style. To the left is the Armory Building, itself changed to an adobe-looking building that became today's History Library (and exhibits area), a part of the Museum of New Mexico. To its left is the Palace of the Governors. The trees in the distance are on the Plaza.

Photo by Jesse Nusbaum; courtesy of the Museum of New Mexico (negative no. 56603)

Chapter Seven
1912-1940:

Santa Fe Style

"The deadly monotony of 10,000 American towns." That's how Carlos Vierra, the early twentieth-century Santa Fe painter and architect and one of the prime movers behind the drive for a city reconverted to "Santa Fe style," described the rest of America in 1917.

Early in the century, a group of Santa Fe men—painters, architects, businessmen, writers, and politicians—decided that there must be a dramatic reversal of building styles in Santa Fe. They opposed the use of any styles that were not considered by them to be Southwestern, such as Victorian and Queen Anne, although by the time this movement began there were many such buildings in Santa Fe—and they'd been there for many years.

The men in this movement proposed that new buildings be constructed in what was called Spanish-Pueblo Revival style, which, in Santa Fe, at least, is also referred to as Santa Fe style.

The movement got off the ground with the erection of the New Mexico State Exposition Building at the San Diego Exposition in 1914 which celebrated the inauguration of the Panama Canal. The state building, modeled after the old missions at Acoma, Zia, and Laguna pueblos, was the model for the present Museum of Fine Arts on the Plaza in Santa Fe.

The building was a huge success and created much comment. Its proponents then sought to spread its style throughout Santa Fe, especially to the public buildings, and to "correct" the styles deemed "non-Southwestern."

By the end of World War I, the Museum of Fine Arts had been built on the northwest corner of the Plaza, and just a few years later, the new LaFonda anchored the southeast corner in a building of strikingly similar features. Both buildings also incorporated interior features which have since become standard in many fine Santa Fe homes, such as exposed *vigas*, deliberately uneven walls, and *kiva*-style fireplaces. Other buildings of the same style erected in a matter of a few years before and after the museum was built included the New Mexico School for the Deaf on Cerrillos Road; the Federal Building on Cathedral Place (then the U.S. Post Office); and the Gross-Kelly and Company Almacen building next to the Denver and Rio Grande depot. (All these buildings are standing today.)

Many other buildings over the years have been changed to conform to the standards set by these proponents, and underneath the adobe brown, the stucco plaster, and the features proposed by these men (see below) are many buildings in Santa Fe today which are, in reality, brick, stone, or cement-block structures that originally had distinct features of other architectural styles.

Witness this example of a change in the atmosphere: In 1873, the *New Mexican* had this to say: "Col. Wm. Breeden has the credit of putting in the first bay window in Santa Fe. It is a handsome, attractive and useful addition to the house." This referred to the Tully house on Grant Avenue. In 1913, however, at the launching of a chamber of commerce architectural prize contest to encourage Santa Fe style plans for houses, one of several requirements was "no bay windows."

Other requirements in that contest included flat foots (a flat roof-pitched roof controversy continues today); an overall effect of a long-low house rather than a high-narrow one; an adobe, lime, or cement finish; color tones in a cream/brown/reddish-brown range; no columns, etc. in the "classic order"; no visible tin roofs; no picket fences. Mention was also made that buildings in the contest should not be constructed in the California Mission style, which was invented well over a century after Santa Fe was founded.

There was resistance to the change from those who liked the styles these people did not, and from those who complained that they were raised in "mud houses" (adobe)—and who didn't want to return to the same. But the movement grew and overwhelmed most of the opposition.

Today, a few examples of unreconstructed Victorian or other "non-Southwest" styles remain in Santa Fe, but a great diversity of architectural styles is lacking because of this twentieth-century movement to rid Santa Fe of anything that did not look, to certain people, to belong in Santa Fe.

Santa Fe style, whether or not one agrees with its imposition on the town, is very different, when contrasted to the architecture of the "10,000" other towns that Vierra mentioned. It is that very style which attracts the visitor and which has caused a lot of them to take a second look—and decide to move to the small capital filled with adobe-brown buildings, no matter that some of them are secretly Victorian with their curlicues plastered over.

Masonic Window

Out of the windows of the Scottish Rite Cathedral could be seen the Palace Hotel, and behind it St. Francis Cathedral, in this photo, taken circa 1912, which would have been one year after the construction of the large pink building that was supposed to resemble Spain's Alhambra.

Photo by Jesse Nusbaum; courtesy of the Museum of New Mexico (negative no. 61382)

Postcard "mystery"

The West was indeed a "mystery" to most Americans before the building of the railroad. This postcard pointed out some of the attractions of Santa Fe to the burgeoning tourist trade.

Photo courtesy of Richard Levy and the Silver Sunbeam, Albuquerque

Rapp Home

I. H. Rapp, architect for the Museum of Fine Arts and a proponent of Santa Fe style, lived here on East Palace Avenue in 1912 before that style became popular. Rapp vowed, in fact, not to build anything in Santa Fe that wasn't in the "traditional" style. He and another architect, Charles Gaastra, were known as "progressive" architects for this adherence to Spanish-Pueblo Revival or Santa Fe style. (Those in the photo are probably members of the Rapp family.)

Photo by Jesse Nusbaum; courtesy of the Museum of New Mexico (negative no. 61489)

1912 Movie

In 1912 Hollywood was already interested in Santa Fe. Here, a photographer from the budding film capital stands at Rosario Cemetery filming the deVargas entrada *at that year's Corpus Christi celebration. Movie companies have used New Mexico, and sometimes the Santa Fe area, for films in more recent years, too.*

Photo courtesy of the Museum of New Mexico (negative no. 10793)

Governor's Mansion

The Governor's Mansion, built in 1907-09, stood near the capitol, erected in 1900. Many administrations used this mansion until it was torn down in the early 1950s. The present mansion, its immediate successor, was opened in 1955.

Photo by T. Harmon Parkhurst; courtesy of the Museum of New Mexico (negative no. 14010)

Manhattan House

Sometime earlier in this century, when Bull Durham tobacco was fifteen cents for two bags, this photo was made at 807 Manhattan Street, where a vacant lot is today. The house was territorial style. "Territorial" houses and other buildings are characterized by brick coping; the use of milled lumber, especially in sawed posts; and triangular wooden window lintels and door frames.

Photo courtesy of the Museum of New Mexico (negative no. 15407)

Capital Interior

Although the exterior of the 1900 capitol was altered beyond recognition in the early 1950s, parts of the interior were left undisturbed. Even today, in parts of the Bataan Building, one sees hallways decorated much this way. Here, however, *in 1912, spittoons along the hallways were not decorative or "period pieces," but real-life necessities.*

Photo by Jesse Nusbaum; courtesy of the Museum of New Mexico (negative no. 61412)

Masonic Interior

Inside the massive, pink Scottish Rite Cathedral at the corner of Paseo de Peralta and Bishop's Lodge Road is this auditorium. The intricate decorative touches still very much in evidence today *were first placed here when the building was constructed in 1911.*

Photo courtesy of the Museum of New Mexico (negative no. 23100)

The Santa Fe High School girls' basketball team, the first in the school's history, lined up for this photo with the Federal Building in the background. This 1912 photo was taken on the high school grounds. The team, coached by Professor Lougee, included (not in identifiable order): Miriam Cartwright, Annie Kaune, Ruth Safford, Dorothy Safford, Consuelo Bergere, Dorothy Goebel, Helen Winter (captain), Adela Miller, and Alta Sanford.

Photo courtesy of Consuelo Bergere Mendenhall

Pflueger Store

With a palm tree in the front, John Pflueger conducted business in his shoe store at 106½ West San Francisco Street. This picture, made in 1912, showed the store two years after Pflueger bought it from Charles Haspelmath. Pflueger was born in Regensburg, Germany, and came to America in 1882, when he was seventeen. He worked at a number of businesses in New Mexico before establishing this store. He was also Santa Fe postmaster about the time this photo was made. The Pflueger store remains in family hands at DeVargas Shopping Mall today.

Photo courtesy of Hansel Pflueger

Bronson Cutting

Bronson Cutting, shown here with his father and mother, Mr. and Mrs. Byard Cutting, and two sisters, a Mrs. Ward and Olivia Cutting, was yet another well-to-do person suffering from tuberculosis who came to Santa Fe for health reasons. In 1912 he acquired the New Mexican; in 1927 he was appointed U.S. senator from New Mexico when Senator A. A. Jones died in office. Cutting remained in the Senate until his death in a plane crash in 1935. His pink residence at 908 Old Santa Fe Trail is now a law firm and private residence.

Photo courtesy of the Museum of New Mexico (negative no. 7118)

Flores Studio

This card advertising the Flores Studio in "Old" Santa Fe shows Seligman Brothers and Spitz Jewelers on the south side of the Plaza; the Spitz store was a landmark with its clock. Today, a newer version of this clock stands in front of the Fine Arts Museum. The Spitz store opened in 1881; in front of the early store was a clock without works. Near the turn of the century, it was replaced by a real clock that was knocked down in 1915 by one of the first motor trucks in Santa Fe.

The clock in front of the museum today is the third clock, purchased secondhand by Salamon Spitz in 1916 from a store in Kansas City. When the portal on the south side of the Plaza was built in 1967, the clock was removed. In 1974 it was installed in its present location, a gift to the city of Santa Fe by Bernard Spitz, Salamon's son. The burros laden with firewood were still a common sight in Santa Fe very early in this century.

Photo courtesy of the State Records Center and Archives, Adella Collier Collection

Holy Faith

Santa Fe in English translates as "Holy Faith," the name of the Episcopal church on East Palace Avenue. This Folk Gothic structure (shown here in 1912) was erected in 1882, two years after the church was renamed (by L. Bradford Prince) to reflect its connection with the territorial capital. It was founded in 1868 as the Good Shepherd Mission, then was renamed St. Thomas after receiving a gift of $1,000 from an anonymous member of a New York City parish of the same name. Additions to the structure shown here were made in 1927 (Palen Hall, the parish hall); 1954 (choir and sanctuary); and 1966 (Conkey House, offices, classrooms, a library, and a chapel).

Photo by Jesse Nusbaum; courtesy of the Museum of New Mexico (negative no. 61359)

New West Academy

The New West Academy (right) occupied the former headquarters of the "Protestant, Christian" University of New Mexico building in this 1912 photo. This building, much altered and re-altered, today is named University Plaza and contains shops and offices. In the background is the 1900 state capitol. The photographer, Jesse Nusbaum, took this picture looking east on Garfield Street at the corner of Guadalupe Street.

Photo courtesy of the Museum of New Mexico (negative no. 11136)

Presbyterian Church (Brick)

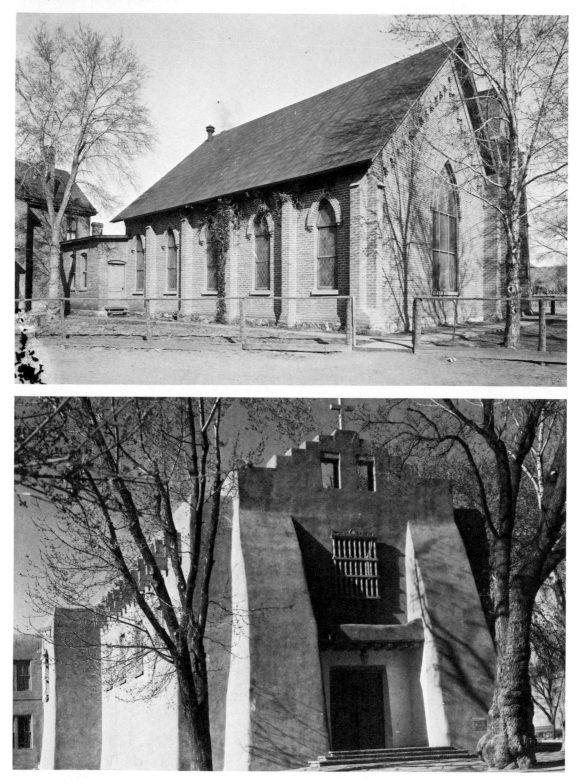

Presbyterian Church (Santa Fe style)

The Presbyterian church in 1912 (above) had not yet been converted to Santa Fe style. Below, a more recent picture shows what the church (with the original brick building underneath) looks like today. The Presbyterians also had the Presbyterian Mission School behind the church building; it was one of the few Protestant schools in Santa Fe.

Photo above by Jesse Nusbaum (negative no. 61360); below by T. Harmon Parkhurst (negative no. 51307); both courtesy of the Museum of New Mexico

Sunmount Interior

At Sunmount Sanitarium in 1913, the residents had quarters such as these. Sunmount was built to cater to those who came to Santa Fe for their health. Many stayed, however, to lead productive, active lives that enhanced the town culturally and socially.

Photo by Jesse Nusbaum; courtesy of the Museum of New Mexico (negative no. 61398)

Business College

The Santa Fe Business College occupied the upper floor of much of the west side of the Plaza in 1913.

Photo by Aaron Craycraft; courtesy of the Museum of New Mexico (negative no. 57095)

Hewett Portrait

E. L. Hewett left the presidency of Highlands University in Las Vegas, New Mexico, to come to Santa Fe in 1909 to become the first director of the Museum of New Mexico. He brought Kenneth Chapman, who had taught at Highlands,

to Santa Fe to work at the museum. At the museum also was a Julian Martinez. Martinez studied the ancient designs in the pottery collection and put that knowledge to work when he later decorated the pots made by his wife, Maria Martinez, probably the most famous Indian potter of this century.

Hewett was responsible for the erection of the Museum of Fine Arts on the site of Fort Marcy army barracks. He also served as the director of the School of American Research when it was affiliated with the museum system. He was the director of the exhibits of science and art at the Panama-California Exposition in San Diego where the New Mexico building caused such an excitement; it was a direct predecessor to the Museum of Fine Arts building. Hewett worked for the preservation of antiquities and helped write federal laws for such preservation.

Photo by the Vreeland Studio at the Panama-California Exposition; courtesy of the Museum of New Mexico (negative no. 7337)

Film with Politicians

These men posed rather stiffly for the movie camera in 1914 for a one-minute film called Santa Fe Politicians. This is a still from that movie. Other Santa Feans in the background enjoying themselves on the Plaza are oblivious to the filmmaker.

Photo courtesy of the State Records Center and Archives, Historic Film Collection, gift of Edward Pigeon

Track Team

The Santa Fe High School track team prepares to run on the school athletic grounds in front of the Federal Building, circa 1914.

Photo courtesy of Consuelo Bergere Mendenhall

Graduating Class, 1914

Six-sevenths of the 1914 graduating class of Santa Fe High School posed for this senior-year photo. From left to right: Eul-Adine Carden, Hansel Pflueger, Consuelo Bergere, Antonio Lucero, Helen Winter, and Elmer Friday. Not pictured (perhaps he was the photographer) was Edward Cartwright.

Photo courtesy of Consuelo Bergere Mendenhall

115

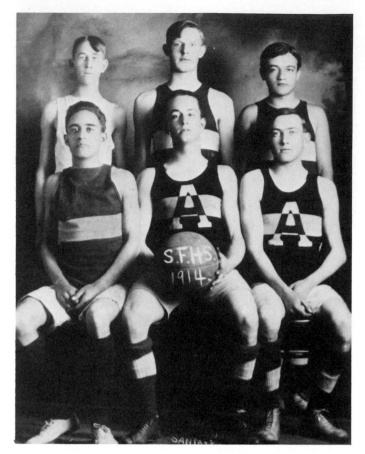

SFHS Boys' Basketball Team

These six young stalwarts posed for the 1914 boys' basketball team photo of Santa Fe High School. The school was then located in the block now containing the Sweeney Convention Center and City Hall.

Photo by Gray Studio; courtesy of Consuelo Bergere Mendenhall

Lamy Statue Dedication

Almost equidistant between New Mexico statehood and the U.S. entry into World War I was this dedication of the statue of the late Archbishop Jean Baptiste Lamy in front of the church he built, St. Francis Cathedral. Lamy, subject of the Willa Cather book, Death Comes for the Archbishop, *was described by Cather as looking "well-bred and distinguished.... There was about him something fearless and fine." After the cathedral was completed, La Parroquia, still standing inside it, was torn down. The rubble from the old adobe church was used to fill in the area in front of the cathedral—the very area where this statue was placed.*

Photo courtesy of the Museum of New Mexico (negative no. 50949)

Company F

Company F lined up in front of the armory (on the right) and the east side of the Palace of the Governors (left) in 1914, the first year of World War I. The armory was later converted to a building in the Museum of New Mexico system, the History Library and exhibits area, and attached to the Palace.

Photo courtesy of Consuelo Bergere Mendenhall

Gazebo

Around 1915 these young people posed in a gazebo that stood on Fort Marcy Hill overlooking Santa Fe. This gazebo, actually a bandstand, had stood in the Plaza for more than thirty years before being removed to Fort Marcy Hill. After a few years on the hill, it was removed and presumably disposed of.

Photo courtesy of the State Records Center and Archives, Adella Collier Collection

Rosario Chapel

Rosario Chapel circa 1915 had exposed adobe bricks, as did many other buildings in Santa Fe at that time. The portion of the church visible here on the left is the original chapel, built in 1807. The year before this photo was taken, the much larger addition to the right was built. Today, in front of an altar screen made by Eugenie Shonnard, a Santa Fe sculptor who studied in Paris under Auguste Rodin, La Conquistadora *rests after she is brought here during the annual Corpus Christi celebration. After several days, she is then returned to her home in her chapel within St. Francis Cathedral.*

Photo courtesy of the Museum of New Mexico (negative no. 10072)

East San Francisco Street

Always a landmark, the St. Francis Cathedral almost appears to be looking down East San Francisco Street at the passersby in this early twentieth-century photo. To the left, the building with a flagpole is the city building that was later moved to the corner of Marcy and Washington streets. The Exchange Hotel is to the right.

Photo by T. Harmon Parkhurst; courtesy of the Museum of New Mexico (negative no. 12158)

May Day

Perhaps this is a May Day celebration in front of the Federal Courthouse in one of the early decades of this century. A few dance to the enjoyment of a large number of Santa Feans who had gathered for the event. The people are standing on public-school grounds now used by the city of Santa Fe.

Photo by T. Harmon Parkhurst; courtesy of the Museum of New Mexico (negative no. 51285)

Soldier

He scarcely looked old enough to fight, but that's probably what he did, no doubt in World War I, or with Brigadier-General John "Black Jack" Pershing's military expedition near—and into—Old Mexico in 1916 after Mexican revolutionaries, under the command of Francisco Villa, had raided Columbus, New Mexico, and killed several soldiers and civilians. G. C. Kaadt Studios caught this wistful, innocent look on the young soldier's face.

Photo courtesy of the State Records Center and Archives, Adella Collier Collection

Panorama of Santa Fe

The former Governor's Mansion is in the foreground of this panorama of Santa Fe, winter 1916. Left-rear is the Federal Courthouse; St. Francis Cathedral is near the center. Between the Courthouse and the cathedral is the Palace Hotel and W. H. Goebel Hardware. Right of the cathedral is Loretto Academy for Girls, and to its right are San Miguel Chapel and St. Michael's College. The photo was taken from the state capitol.

Photo courtesy of the Museum of New Mexico (negative nos. 10144 and 10148)

White House Store

The Catron building has housed a variety of department stores on its ground floor. The White House had been there for four years when this July 9, 1916, photo was taken. That store was owned by Johanna Uhlfelder Blatt and her husband Morris Blatt and occupied the site of the present-day Guarantee store. The building is marked "Catron Block" (and still contains the Catron law firm

on the top floor), but it is often called the Blatt Building by Santa Feans.

Photo by Anna L. Hase; courtesy of the Museum of New Mexico (negative no. 16512)

Movie Still

A 1916 movie, Trip to Santa Fe, *took viewers around the old town. This was shot on West San Francisco Street, between Galisteo Street and Don Gaspar Avenue, looking east, towards the cathedral.*

Photo courtesy of the State Records Center and Archives

Claire Hotel

The Claire Hotel stood on the southwest corner of the Plaza (now the site of the Ore House restaurant) when this photo was taken in 1916. The street on the left is San Francisco Street. In the Claire can be seen the firm of Renehan and Wright; the law offices of E. R. Davies; and the office of Dr. DeForest Lord, a dentist. W. H. Crist Levy's saloon was on this corner in 1913. Also to be seen are Kerr's barbershop and the Capital City Bank, which failed circa 1922.

Photo by Theodore Asplund; courtesy of the Museum of New Mexico (negative no. 10671)

A May Day Parade

A May Day school parade circa 1916-17 went past the Felipe B. Delgado house on West Palace Avenue. The house is now owned by the Historic Santa Fe Foundation and is leased to New Mexico Banquest Corporation.

Photo by Theodore Asplund; courtesy of the Museum of New Mexico (negative no. 10968)

John Dendahl

John Dendahl, a member of the third generation of Dendahls to grace Santa Fe, posed around 1917-18 for photographer Wesley Bradfield. The Dendahl family home is now an office building between Cookworks and the Swiss Palace Bakery at 318 Guadalupe Street. John's grandfather, also named John, came to Santa Fe from Germany, and his father Henry, born in Santa Fe in 1888, was a 1905 graduate of Santa Fe High School (with three other seniors). The store of the same name is still in business in Santa Fe

and is now located in the Solana Shopping Center on West Alameda Street.

Photo courtesy of the Museum of New Mexico (negative no. 13443)

Sanatorium Sign

The gate to St. Vincent Sanatorium on Cathedral Place is still there, minus the sign, well over half a century after this January 1917 photo was taken. Now the St. Vincent Auxiliary holds an annual fair in this location to raise money for the present hospital, a "descendant" of the other hospitals and sanatorium of the same name.

Photo by Anna L. Hase; courtesy of the Museum of New Mexico (negative no. 15219)

Shopper

West San Francisco Street was popular with shoppers around 1918—as it is now. Residents could find pretty much what other Americans could find in their stores, yet tourists were already being catered to with a preponderance of Indian and Spanish items, such as weavings, pottery, and baskets.

This young woman, caught at the corner of San Francisco Street and Don Gaspar Avenue, may have been on her way to shop or to work, since many jobs formerly held by men were being occupied by women during World War I. Incidentally, New Mexico and Arizona had brought the stars in that flag up to forty-eight only six years before.

Photo courtesy of the Museum of New Mexico (negative no. 14142)

Red Cross

These girls in their miniature Red Cross uniforms helped bring a bit of cheer to a World War I-era crowd around the Plaza circa 1918.

Posed here were, left to right, Elreena and Corrine Arrighi. The Arrighi family had the Parlor Meat Market on West San Francisco Street and the Del Rio Meat Market on Galisteo Street (occupying part of the present location of the Tiano Sporting Goods store).

Photo by Wesley Bradfield; courtesy of the Museum of New Mexico (negative no. 14079)

Sugar Demo

Doing their part for the war effort, these young Santa Fe women were demonstrating how to conserve sugar. In this *photo, taken around 1918, the last year of the war, the women prepared to share with other Santa Feans ways to use less of* *the then-scarce commodity.*

Photo courtesy of the Museum of New Mexico (negative no. 14075)

Armistice Day

On the first Armistice Day (1918), a crowd on Lincoln Avenue gathered for the burning in effigy of Kaiser Wilhelm. War fever had run high in Santa Fe and anti-German feeling had also been very strong. In fact, such German-born, prominent Santa Feans as John Dendahl and John Pflueger had been reluctant to be seen in public speaking to one another—even in English, so the old friends had to meet secretly.

Photo by Wesley Bradfield; courtesy of the Museum of New Mexico (negative no. 59825)

Nordfeldt

B. J. O. Nordfeldt, Norwegian by birth, was one of many artists who moved to Santa Fe during the 1910s and 1920s. Nordfeldt first arrived in 1918 and came back again and again to paint during the next twenty years. He stood in front of a self-portrait for this photograph.

Photo courtesy of the Museum of New Mexico (negative no. 7744)

Vierra House

Carlos Vierra designed a house at 1002 Old Pecos Trail that was to set a trend for others interested in building in the Spanish-Pueblo Revival style. He incorporated vigas *(ceiling supports that protruded through the exterior of the house);* corbels *(decorative wooden pieces that joined the pillars and the cross beams); rounded corners; and, of course, adobe. The house was financed by Frank Springer, an attorney and regent of the Museum of New Mexico, who also paid for much of the construction costs of the Museum of Fine Arts built around this same time. Vierra lived in the house owned by Springer with the understanding that he could do so for the remainder of his life, which he did. After his death his wife moved away from Santa Fe.*

Photo courtesy of the Museum of New Mexico (negative no. 10557)

Gross-Kelly

Gross-Kelly and Company was one of the first firms to make use of the Santa Fe style architecture, better known as Spanish-Pueblo Revival. This building, designed by the Rapp architectural firm, made use of the "approved" styles of the new wave sweeping Santa Fe. It was constructed in 1914. Gross-Kelly and Company was a retail-wholesale mercantile firm that had business in several states and Mexico from 1902 to 1954. It was preceded by two firms: Otero-Sellar, which existed from 1867 to 1881; and Gross-Blackwell, from 1881 to 1902.

The story of the companies and the families associated with them is told in The Buffalo Head by Daniel T. Kelly, Sr. (with Santa Fe historian Beatrice Chauvenet). The title comes from a buffalo head that was donated to Otero-Sellar and Company by Grand Duke Alexis of Russia in 1880, when he hunted in the West. The head is now in the Harvard Club in New York.

Photo courtesy of the State Records Center and Archives, gift of Ron Passarelli

Hogel Store

The W. H. Hogel store was at the corner of Manhattan and College streets in 1918-20. By 1922 Mr. Hogel had a home furnishings store in Galisteo, south of Santa Fe.

Photo courtesy of the Museum of New Mexico (negative no. 31632)

Manderfield Home

Miss Eugenia Manderfield (left), daughter of William H. Manderfield, publisher of the New Mexican (1863-81), sat in her garden with a friend circa 1918. The Manderfield home has since been torn down. It stood south of the present Bull Ring restaurant on Old Santa Fe Trail.

Photo courtesy of the Museum of New Mexico (negative no. 10532)

Sloan Painting

John Sloan painted Under the Old Portal, *a Santa Fe scene owned today by the Museum of Fine Arts, a building that is not far from the locale of this work. Sloan, who achieved world prominence as an artist during his lifetime, first came to* Santa Fe in 1919 with Randall Davey, another painter who brought fame to Santa Fe through his work. Sloan spent more than thirty summers in New Mexico in his house on Garcia Street, later occupied by another artist, Chuzo *Tamotzu, until the latters's death in 1975.*

Photo courtesy of the Museum of New Mexico (negative no. 44383)

Governor Prince Residence

Governor L. Bradford Prince, who headed New Mexico from 1889 to 1893, lived in Prince Plaza, just west of Sena Plaza on East Palace Avenue. He purchased the building in 1879 (when he was the newly appointed territorial supreme court justice) from Carmen Benavides de Roubidoux, the widow of Antoine Roubidoux, a French-Canadian trader and interpreter for Brigadier-General Kearny. This 1919 photo contrasts the more traditional horse-and-buggy mode of transportation with the motor car. The majority of Santa Feans used neither one to shop or get to work. They walked, muddy streets and all.

Photo by Charles F. Coffin; courtesy of the Museum of New Mexico (negative no. 88800)

Cross

The Cross of the Martyrs dedicated in 1920 is shown here under construction. Today the neighborhood around this cross is heavily populated, and another cross has been erected on Fort Marcy Hill, above the Santa Fe Girls' Club, by the Fiesta Council. The older cross is located on a hill near the Hayt-Wientge house on the north side of town.

Photo courtesy of the Museum of New Mexico (negative no. 57999)

Exchange Hotel Goes

The old Exchange Hotel, now the site of LaFonda, on the southeastern corner of the Plaza, was destroyed by World War I tanks in 1919 in preparation for the building of the present hotel. Fonda means "inn" in Spanish, and legend has it that a hotel has been on this site almost ever since there's been a Santa Fe. It is known, at least, that a hotel did exist here for most if not all of the nineteenth century.

Persons who wanted to drive the tank had to first buy U. S. Bonds in this combination demolition-bond campaign. One elderly, current resident of Santa Fe described the razing of the hotel as being so "horribly dusty" that she and her friends soon left the site.

Photo courtesy of the State Records Center and Archives, Adella Collier Collection

Bynner Drawing

"Hal," or Witter Bynner, is shown here in a 1910 drawing, before he came to live at Sunmount Sanitarium in Santa Fe—a city he was to make his home for the next several decades. Bynner was born in Brooklyn in 1881. According to a story, he and Eleanor Wilson, the daughter of Woodrow Wilson, danced a version of the Charleston called "Kitchen Sink" at a Grange Hall in New Hampshire, and so shocked the town that the city fathers closed the hall for one year "to punish themselves for allowing such goings-on." Today the Witter Bynner Foundation for Poetry, located in Santa Fe, perpetuates this writer's memory by giving money to literary causes.

Photo courtesy of the State Records Center and Archives

Orphans in Parade

St. Vincent's Orphanage had a contingent in the May 1, 1920, All-American Day Parade, a post-World War I phenomenon in a world shattered by the horrors of that war. To the immediate left is the Governor's Mansion, and the state capitol is in the background. The orphanage (1865-1955) was located behind St. Francis Cathedral and, like the sanatorium and the hospital, run by the Sisters of Charity.

Photo by Wesley Bradfield; courtesy of the Museum of New Mexico (negative no. 51990)

Cross Dedicated

The Cross of the Martyrs was dedicated at the Fiesta in September 1920. The camera faced the town as seen from that northside hill. The cross commemorated the Franciscans killed in the Pueblo Revolt in 1680. The plaque at the base reads, "Erected by members of the Knights of Columbus and the Historical Society of New Mexico in memory of the Franciscan Friars who were killed by the Pueblo Indians in the revolution in the province of New Mexico August 9 and 10 A.D. 1680."

Photo courtesy of the Museum of New Mexico (negative no. 52464)

Twitchell Home

Ralph Emerson Twitchell built this rather fortress-like house on the corner of what is now the Paseo de Peralta and Grant Avenue. Twitchell was a proponent of the Santa Fe style, and his house reflects this. The house was torn down circa 1970.

Photo by T. Harmon Parkhurst; courtesy of the Museum of New Mexico (negative no. 13412)

Nash

Willard Nash was one of the Cinco Pintores, or "five painters" who helped put Santa Fe on the map as an artists' colony. The others were Will Shuster, Josef Bakos, Walter Mruk, and Fremont Ellis. The group was formed in 1921 and lasted a few years. All built homes on Camino del Monte Sol (dubbed "the five nuts in five mud huts"), an area that became a favorite of the many artists and writers to make Santa Fe their home. Ellis arrived in 1919, Mruk probably arrived in 1920, Shuster circa 1918, Bakos in 1921, and Nash in 1920.

Photo courtesy of the Museum of New Mexico (negative no. 95289)

Abe Spiegelberg

"Abe" Spiegelberg, a member of one of the prominent nineteenth-century German-Jewish merchant families, is captured here (left) by the brush of Josef Bakos, one of the Cinco Pintores, in 1921, and (right) by the lens of Jesse Nusbaum circa 1912.

Nusbaum photo (negative no. 28790) and Bakos portrait (negative no. 28819) courtesy of the Museum of New Mexico

Fremont Ellis

Fremont Ellis, the last survivor of the Cinco Pintores, *arrived in Santa Fe in the summer of 1919, the date of this photo, which shows him on San Francisco Street, just west of the Big Jo Lumber Company. Ellis, who grew up in many* locations around the country, fell in love with Santa Fe—as did many artists. After a walk through the town and in the surrounding hills, he was rhapsodizing about his love affair with Santa Fe to Abe Spiegelberg, the local merchant. During his enthusiastic report on his walk, Spiegelberg kept shaking his head. Finally, Ellis asked him what was wrong. "You came too late," Spiegelberg said. The Spiegelberg family had come to Santa Fe when the Anglo-Americans arrived in 1846.*

Photo courtesy of Fremont Ellis

Mruk

W. E. Mruk, one of the Cinco Pintores, *stood in front of the Museum of Fine Arts' massive doors in 1921. The light and color in and around Santa Fe attracted many artists; other attractions for them were the faces and bearing of the Pueblo Indians and the Hispanics. The liberal policies of the Museum of Fine Arts in providing studio space and sometimes monetary compensation helped establish Santa Fe as a foremost center for artists.*

Photo by Wesley Bradfield; courtesy of the Museum of New Mexico (negative no. 32333)

132

Oñate Theatre

Santa Feans in 1921 gathered on the Plaza for a parade in front of Cassell's Oñate Theatre building, now the site of the First National Bank, where Paramount Week was being featured with a rash of silent movies. The building was one of the earliest Spanish-Pueblo Revival buildings, complete with decorative ladders resembling those still used at such authentic adobe structures as Taos Pueblo, north of the city. To the right was the Cassell Motor Company, a garage.

The theater was also known as El Casa de los Conquistadores and contained large wall murals painted by Gerald Cassidy. They depicted the meeting of Coronado and the Zuni Indians in 1540. Those murals, restored, are now in the lobby of the main post office building on Federal Place. The theater was replaced by the Smart Shop in 1929.

Photo courtesy of the Museum of New Mexico (negative no. 10661)

Gerald Cassidy Home

Gerald Cassidy, an architect and painter who moved to Santa Fe in the 1910s, redesigned an old house at 924 Canyon Road. This portal on the patio incorporated a carved choir loft beam from the collapsed Nambe Mission Church north of Santa Fe. The church had been built around 1725.

Photo courtesy of the Museum of New Mexico (negative no. 91638)

Cassidy Five

Gerald Cassidy became his own Cinco Pintores in this image by the Marlborough Photo Shop. Cassidy was a leading figure in the art world of Santa Fe and helped promote the Spanish-Pueblo Revival style of architecture. His wife, Ina Sizer Cassidy, was a writer who published widely on the arts and artists of the town.

Photo courtesy of the Museum of New Mexico (negative no. 37734)

Cassidy Mural

Painted in 1921 by Gerald Cassidy for the Oñate Theatre on the Plaza, this large mural and its companion showing Coronado and his men are now in the main post office building lobby.

Photo courtesy of the Museum of New Mexico (negative no. 20205)

St. Mike's Baseball

These little boys formed one of the baseball teams representing St. Michael's College in 1922. Today, St. Mike's is outflanked numerically by Santa Fe High School, but a strong loyalty to the Catholic school is found in Santa Fe because of the large number of alumni who remain Santa Feans.

Photo courtesy of the Christian Brothers and St. Michael's High School

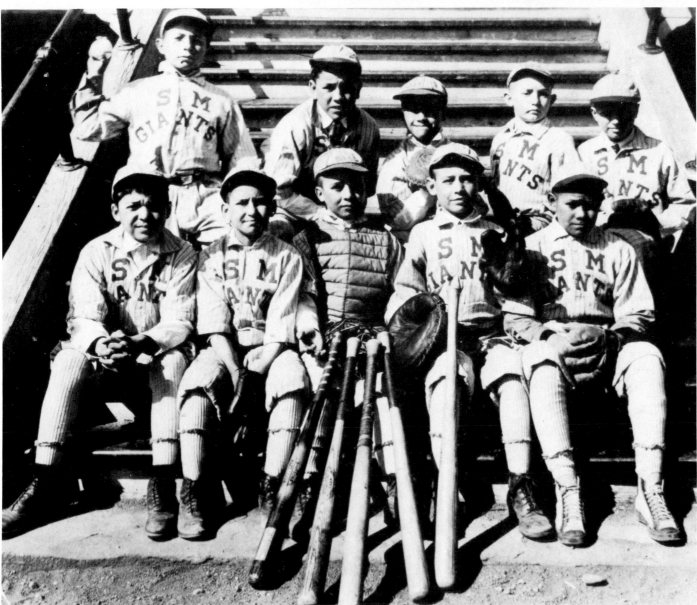

Davey Dressing Room

Randall Davey, one of the artists attracted to Santa Fe, designed his wife's dressing room in their Canyon Road home. This house was originally a sawmill, built by the U.S. Army quartermaster in 1847. It was sold at a public auction in 1852 (along with a lot of other land and buildings) to Colonel Ceran St. Vrain. After going through several other owners, including descendants of Nicolás Ortiz III, the house was acquired by Davey in 1920. He occupied it for more than forty years, until his fatal automobile accident.

Photo by T. Harmon Parkhurst; courtesy of the Museum of New Mexico (negative no. 32104)

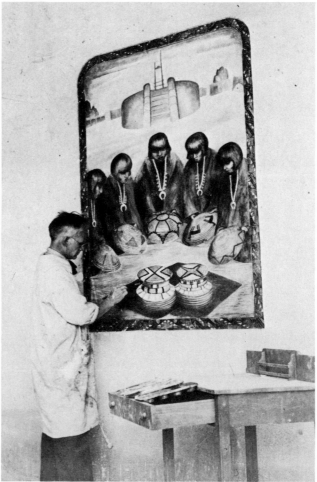

Shuster Mural

Will Shuster painted the murals in the Museum of Fine Arts patio. The Indians—their faces, dress, pottery, pueblos and dances—were themes of many of the Santa Fe artists; such themes continue to be important to many area artists today.

Photo by R. H. Dawson; courtesy of the Museum of New Mexico (negative no. 30849)

Parsons

Sheldon Parsons was one of the first artists to move to Santa Fe. He came with his daughter Sarah in 1913. They lived for a time in the Padre Gallegos house on Washington Avenue, and also in Gerald Cassidy's house at 924 Canyon Road after Cassidy bought the house in 1915, the same year this photo was made. Parsons, along with Carlos Vierra, William Penhallow Henderson, Edgar Lee Hewett, Alice Corbin Henderson, Gerald Cassidy, and Ralph Emerson Twitchell, helped revive the Santa Fe Fiesta in 1919.

Photo courtesy of the Museum of New Mexico (negative no. 7822)

Henderson Painting

William Penhallow Henderson and his wife, Alice Corbin Henderson, came to Santa Fe in 1916 to live at Sunmount Sanitarium for health reasons. Like so many others who came here to seek a cure, they fell in love with Santa Fe and remained. They were among those who promoted the Santa Fe Fiesta in 1919. William Penhallow Henderson's painting Santa Fe Plaza *is shown here. The town itself was often the subject of paintings by the early artists. Renowned San Ildefonso Pueblo artists Maria and Julian Martinez posed for the central figures in this painting. It was one of those on exhibit at the opening of the Fine Arts Museum in 1917. It is now in the collection of Robert E. McKee III.*

The Hendersons' daughter, Alice Henderson Rossin, opened a specialty shop in Santa Fe in 1933, Todas Cosas, or "All Things," which featured denim and bandana creations that were soon being sold in fashionable dress shops around the country and which helped set a trend for such fashions—and put Santa Fe on the map one more time. Rossin's son-in-law, cartoonist Bill Mauldin of the Chicago Sun-Times, *is another member of the family to claim Santa Fe as home.*

Photo courtesy of the Museum of New Mexico (negative no. 35482)

Moving Building

What seemed impossible to many Santa Feans actually happened in 1922: this city building was moved from what is now the Federal Building parking lot on East San Francisco Street to the present site of the Berardinelli Building at the corner of Washington and Marcy. The moving of this building caused quite a stir in a town not accustomed to the wholesale removal of a substantial brick building from one location to another. Fifteen years after the building reached its new location, it was torn down for the construction of the Berardinelli Building.

Photo courtesy of the Museum of New Mexico (negative no. 14014)

Fiesta Cowboys and Indians

Some Indians and cowboys staged entertainment on the grounds of the Palace Hotel during a Fiesta in the early 1920s.

Photo courtesy of the State Records Center and Archives, E. Boyd Collection

DePalma

"Napoleon & De Palma, Manufacture's of Monuments, Mausoleums and Memorials" was located on Galisteo Street when this 1922 photo was made, one year after Charles De Palma founded the firm. De Palma is standing in the doorway with his arms folded. The firm also made the stone walls and carved arches and gates around Rosario Cemetery, and the church at Lamy, New Mexico, southeast of Santa Fe. The shop closed around 1926.

Photo courtesy of Domenic C. De Palma

Jonson

Raymond Jonson moved to Santa Fe in 1924 (two years after his first visit) and taught as well as painted in the town until 1949. He settled on Camino de las Animas, off College Street, an area where many of the early artists lived. Later, Canyon Road and Camino del Monte Sol (often dubbed simply "the Camino") were the popular places to live for many of the Santa Fe artists.

Photo by T. Harmon Parkhurst; courtesy of the Museum of New Mexico (negative no. 73928)

Balink and Martinez

Henry Balink, (left) came to America from his native Holland and became one of the first painters to arrive in Santa Fe, settling on Old Pecos Trail in 1917. His son Henry now operates an art studio on Old Santa Fe Trail. Balink is shown here with Juan Martinez of Taos Pueblo, the man who posed for Gerald Cassidy's mural of the Zuni Indians that now hangs in the main post office lobby.

Photo courtesy of the Museum of New Mexico (negative no. 36354)

Fiesta Amphitheatre

Santa Fe had a Fiesta amphitheatre on the north side of town in 1926 when these people gathered for a Fiesta celebration. Note the Scottish Rite Cathedral to the right, and the Allison-James School (which became the Santa Fe Business College in 1938) further to the right.

Photo courtesy of the State Records Center and Archives, John Gaw Meem Collection

Adelina Otero-Warren

The author of Spain in Our Southwest, *Adelina "Nina" Otero-Warren, posed against a tree sometime early in this century. The author moved to Santa Fe as a young woman, but was born at Los Lunas, the ancestral home of her mother, Eloisa Luna. She was an unsuccessful candidate for the U. S. Congress in the 1930s.*

Photo courtesy of Consuelo Bergere Mendenhall

Palace Drawing

The Palace Hotel, built in 1880, was to have been changed to look like this drawing, an effort to make it, too, conform to the wave of buildings being converted to a Spanish-Pueblo Revival style. The building burned down before the owners could complete the conversion, although some of the changes had been made at the time of the demise of the hotel. In its last years, it was known as the DeVargas Hotel, not to be confused with the one now on Don Gaspar Avenue.

Photo courtesy of the Museum of New Mexico (negative no. 61428)

Palace Fire

Under mysterious circumstances, the Palace Hotel burned down in 1922. It was suspected, but never proved, that someone had started the fire.

Photo courtesy of the State Records Center and Archives, Adella Collier Collection

LaFonda Entertainment

Entertainment at LaFonda gave tourists what they came to see—plenty of Spanish and Indian dancing and costumes. There was nothing like it back home. Here, one of the Spanish dancers struck a dramatic pose.

Photo by Fine Arts Studio, El Paso, Texas; courtesy of the Museum of New Mexico (negative no. 55474)

Tea in Portal

Tea in the south portal of LaFonda was a social occasion obviously enjoyed by these women in the 1920s. LaFonda provided a long list of comforts and entertainments for the visitor. Fred Harvey took over the construction and management of this hotel after local capital gave out and made it part of his chain of outstanding hotels along and near the Santa Fe Railroad. His Harvey-cars carried guests to outlying Indian pueblos and natural wonders, then brought them back for tea—and a feverish comparing of notes.

Photo by T. Harmon Parkhurst; courtesy of the Museum of New Mexico (negative no. 54316)

Harveycar and Capitol

A Harveycar, full of "dudes," came to a stop in front of the state capitol on a tour of exotic Santa Fe.

Photo by T. Harmon Parkhurst; courtesy of the Museum of New Mexico (negative no. 10385)

St. Michael's Gym

St. Michael's College students worked out in this gymnasium at the campus on College Street when the school was at its downtown location. Both St. Michael's and Santa Fe High School campuses were downtown for decades, and both moved away from those locations for sites on the south side of the city in recent years. Actually, St. Mike's split into two campuses in 1947 when the college-level classes were moved to what is now the College of Santa Fe location on Cerrillos Road and St. Michael's Drive. The high school remained at the old 1859 site by San Miguel Chapel until the mid-1960s.

Photo courtesy of the Christian Brothers and St. Michael's High School

John Sloan

John Sloan painted one of his landscapes somewhere outside of town in 1926 with wife Dolly in the car. The prominence of such artists in Santa Fe helped attract even more artists to the town.

Photo by T. Harmon Parkhurst; courtesy of the Museum of New Mexico (negative no. 28835)

St. Michael's Group

The St. Michael's College faculty and student body posed for the special camera that took this shot in 1925-26 inside the school grounds. Today, three of these buildings remain: the Lamy Building (shown here with a mansard roof), which lost its top floor to a fire in 1927; the San Miguel Chapel, and the Lew Wallace Building (the large brick building on the right). The camera distorted the buildings so they appear to be curved. Because of such a distortion, the photographer had the students and faculty sit in a curve—so they would appear to be sitting in a straight line.

Photo courtesy of the Christian Brothers and St. Michael's High School

Willa Cather

Willa Cather, author of Death Comes for the Archbishop, a thinly disguised biography of Archbishop Jean Baptiste Lamy, is seen here in Santa Fe with Ralph Emerson Twitchell (left), the attorney-historian, and an unidentified man. Cather wrote much of the Lamy book in Santa Fe in 1926, doing some of her writing at the house of writer Mary Austin and some probably at her room in LaFonda. In Mary Austin's library was an autographed copy of the book (published in 1927) with the inscription, "For Mary Austin, in whose lovely study I wrote the last chapters of this book. She will be my sternest critic—and she has the right to be. I will always take a calling-down from my betters" (Pearce, Literary America).

Feelings about her book remain divided today. While it is recommended reading for anyone interested in Santa Fe, those residents who believe Lamy was too harsh on the nineteenth-century citizens and clergy of the territory feel it is a romanticized tale of the French-born cleric.

Photo courtesy of the Museum of New Mexico (negative no. 7129)

Elks' Club

The Elks' Club on Lincoln Avenue, shown here in 1926, is today part of the Museum of New Mexico complex behind the Palace of the Governors. Today's building lacks much of the ornate decoration shown here.

Photo courtesy of the Museum of New Mexico (negative no. 36885)

Hagerman Home

Herbert J. Hagerman, governor of New Mexico 1906-07, lived in this Lincoln Avenue residence (a former officer's house on the Fort Marcy military complex) in 1926, the year of this photograph. On this site today is the Sears, Roebuck department store.

Photo courtesy of the Museum of New Mexico (negative no. 23107)

Lindy

"Lucky Lindy," Charles Lindbergh, visited Santa Fe on September 25, 1927, in none other than the Spirit of St. Louis, famous in its own right. Here, Lindbergh (right) is shown with Mayor Ed Safford immediately after his landing. His successful solo crossing of the Atlantic had been accomplished only weeks before, on May 20-21.

Photo by Ramona B. Latimer; courtesy of the Museum of New Mexico (negative no. 92077)

Guadalupe Church

This Cadillac stood in front of the late eighteenth-century Guadalupe Church circa 1926-28. The street to the left if Agua Fria Street but was originally El Camino Real ("the royal road") that led from Santa Fe to Mexico City. Across the street to the left was the elementary school attached to this church (now Mercado Hispano del Norte, a collection of shops) and a convent (now La Tertulia restaurant).

Photo by T. Harmon Parkhurst; courtesy of the Museum of New Mexico (negative no. 10038)

Don Gaspar Avenue

Don Gaspar Avenue, looking into the center of town, was the subject of this circa 1927 photo. The DeVargas Hotel, still a familiar landmark, is down on the left.

Photo courtesy of the Museum of New Mexico (negative no. 51490)

First Fiesta Queen

Amalia Sena Sanchez, granddaughter of José Sena who built Sena Plaza, was asked by E. Dana Johnson, editor of the New Mexican, to be the first Fiesta queen in 1927. When she replied that she was married and had children, Mr. Johnson said, "So did Queen Victoria!" She wore the satin bridal gown made for her mother's 1886 wedding. (It has since been worn by Mrs. Sanchez's descendants for their weddings.)

On top of the Santa Fe Ticket Office, across from LaFonda, she was crowned queen by Governor Dillon. Mrs. Mugler of the Mugler Millinery Shop (that had earlier occupied the ticket-office location) made her a crown which is shown here (covered mostly by Mrs. Sanchez's mantilla).

Photo courtesy of Amalia Sena Sanchez

149

Austin and Seton

Mary Austin, writer, first visited Santa Fe in 1918 and lived in the town from 1923 until her death in 1934. In Santa Fe, she entertained many distinguished visitors, including Willa Cather, Vachel Lindsay, Sinclair Lewis, Frances Perkins, Sherwood Anderson, Marianne Moore, H. L. Mencken, Mark Van Doren, Ansel Adams, Ezra Pound, Amy Lowell, Jack London, and the man shown here, Ernest Thompson Seton. She kept up a lively correspondence, too, with a number of other well-known figures that included the Herbert Hoovers. In 1925 she built a large adobe house on Camino del Monte Sol which she named La Casa Querida, "The Beloved House." She lived in it until her death.

Seton Village, outside Santa Fe, is where Ernest Seton built a large house called The Castle (it survives) on a hillside overlooking several other buildings he had constructed. The other buildings were used for nature studies and the training of youth and adults who were members of the Boy Scouts, Campfire Girls, and the Woodcraft League. (Seton was the founder of the Boy Scout movement in the United States.) Seton Village was made a National Historic Landmark in 1947, a year before his death. His vast collection of stuffed animals and birds, artifacts, and his library were given to the Philmont Scout Ranch at Cimarron, New Mexico.

Photo by Carroll Stryker; courtesy of the Museum of New Mexico (negative no. 14348)

Read Street

Read Street, looking east from Guadalupe Street, circa 1928, was the subject of one of a series of photos by the Santa Fe Railway. The Hesch house, one of the few houses remaining in Santa Fe with a mansard roof, is on the right. It was built in 1888.

Photo courtesy of the Museum of New Mexico (negative no. 92247)

Montezuma Street

Another Santa Fe Railway photo of 1928, this time of Montezuma Street, is shown here. The photographer was standing at Guadalupe Street, looking east on Montezuma. The Santa Fe Reporter *now publishes out of the house on the right.*

Photo courtesy of the Museum of New Mexico (negative no. 92223)

Franciscan Hotel

One of the hotels that did not survive until the present time was the Franciscan Hotel, at the corner of Garfield and Guadalupe streets, although the building is still very much in use. This photo, taken in 1928, looks east on Garfield, and shows the building as it was after and before the mansard roof was present. The building was realtered in recent years, and a mansard-roofed tower again appeared. It is now called University Plaza.

Photo courtesy of the Museum of New Mexico (negative no. 92246)

Bynner in Parade

Witter Bynner gave a maniacal pose to the photographer, who caught him in a Fiesta parade around the Plaza in the late 1920s. Bynner was a leading light in the literary community that existed alongside the artistic one in the 1920s and 1930s. Four years before arriving in Santa Fe in 1920 as a "lunger," Bynner and friend Arthur Davison Ficke created a famous literary hoax. They published, under the nom de plume *Emmanuel Morgan (Bynner) and Anne Knish (Ficke), a school of Futurist verse known as "Spectra." The "Spectrists" were taken seriously by the literary world, but when the hoax was discovered, both men were attacked—and never forgiven—by many who had been taken in.*

Photo courtesy of the Museum of New Mexico (negative no. 6999)

151

K. C. Waffle House

The interior of the K. C. Waffle House around 1930 revealed the Southwest motif that tourists wrote home about and which local residents enjoyed in their own homes. The Waffle House, at the northeast corner of Don Gaspar and Water streets, was succeeded by the Mayflower Cafe; then the Golden Temple Conscious Cookery (1974-77); Pogo's Eatery (1977-79); and today it is the home of Pasqual's Restaurant (1978-). Sitting at the counter was Mrs. Gus Mitchell, wife of the proprietor of the Waffle House, and her two daughters.

Photo by T. Harmon Parkhurst; courtesy of the Museum of New Mexico (negative no. 50968)

153

Van Soelen

Theodore Van Soelen posed in front of his painting of his family, Summer Battles. In this photo, circa 1945-46, Van Soelen is also standing in front of a photo of his son Don in his World War II uniform. Don is the boy in the middle in the painting. Ted, his other son, and Jay, his daughter, are also shown. The Van Soelens led a rather conventional life compared to some of the other painters and writers of Santa Fe. Their friends tended to be business people and others not of the art community, although Mr. Van Soelen had a few close friends who were well-known artists, particularly in Santa Fe and nearby Taos.

Van Soelen came originally to New Mexico because of his tubercular condition; he met and married Virginia Morrison Carr (shown in the painting), the daughter of a New Mexico cattle baron and army general, E. A. Carr. They built a house in Tesuque, just north of town, which is now owned by the singer Roger Miller. Van Soelen also wrote for such publications as Field and Stream *and often illustrated those articles.*

Photo courtesy of the State Records Center and Archives

First National

In 1928 the First National Bank stood on what is now the site of the Kiva Trading Post on the east side of the Plaza. In the background to the right is LaFonda.

Photo courtesy of the Museum of New Mexico (negative no. 51875)

Lensic Exterior

The Lensic Theatre, looking pretty much as it does today, was opened in 1930. The building was erected by Nathan Salmon and E. John Greer. On the site of the Lensic Sandwich Shop was Doña Tules's famous monte parlor of the mid-1800s.

Photo by T. Harmon Parkhurst; courtesy of the Museum of New Mexico (negative no. 50969)

Lensic Interior

Today's Santa Feans come into a Lensic Theatre almost as fancy as the one moviegoers entered in 1930, the date of this photo, and the year the theater was opened.

Photo by T. Harmon Parkhurst; courtesy of the Museum of New Mexico (negative no. 50970)

Oliver LaFarge

Oliver LaFarge, after whom a branch of the Santa Fe Public Library is now named, won the Pulitzer Prize in 1931 for his novel about Indian Life, Laughing Boy. *Among LaFarge's many other books is* Santa Fe: The Autobiography of a Southwestern Town, *a collection of memorable clips from the* New Mexican *over a century. LaFarge was a leader in the Indian-rights movement.*

Photo courtesy of the Museum of New Mexico (negative no. 16741)

Seligman Inauguration

Arthur Seligman, second from left on the bench, descendant of one of the nineteenth-century merchant families, became Governor of New Mexico in 1931, replacing Governor Richard C. Dillon. The Seligmans and Dillons, along with members of their families and staffs, posed for this inaugural photo in the Fine Arts Museum.

Photo courtesy of the Museum of New Mexico (negative no. 11020)

Bill Palou

Bill Palou's band on the roof terrace of LaFonda during the Fiesta, circa 1932, provided entertainment not only for hotel guests but for passersby as well. Farolitos, *normally reserved for Christmas-* time, *await the darkness along the ledges and edges of the building.*

Photo courtesy of the State Records Center and Archives, Adella Collier Collection

Library

After the 1932-33 John Gaw Meem remodeling of the old Woman's Board of Trade public library building by the Santa Fe Woman's Club and Library Association, the library on Washington Avenue looked like this. Today, these double doors have become windows, and the entrance is where the left front window is in this photograph.

Photo courtesy of the Museum of New Mexico (negative no. 91339)

157

Staab Building

At 118 West San Francisco Street one could find Z. Staab and Brother when T. Harmon Parkhurst took this photo circa 1933-34. Staab's was one of Santa Fe's older mercantile establishments, founded in the final quarter of the nineteenth century, as the building notes, when many such firms began in Santa Fe.

Photo courtesy of the Museum of New Mexico (negative no. 10778)

Taichert's

Next to Z. Staab and Brother's was Taichert's Variety Store in the Galisteo Building at West San Francisco and Galisteo streets. Upstairs, in room 208, was the B. G. Studio, proprietor Blas Galvan. Rooms 210-214 housed the Democratic State Headquarters. The building also contained offices for the state employment offices in this Depression-era photo (1933-34). Today, Taichert's location is occupied by two stores, Morningbird and C. G. Rein Gallery. Taichert's was also one of the stores in Santa Fe's first shopping center, called Santa Fe Shopping Center, which in 1955 opened in the 2100 block of Cerrillos Road, the present site of Santa Fe Auto Supply and other stores.

Photo courtesy of the Museum of New Mexico (negative no. 50965)

Farolitos

An old tradition in Santa Fe is the lighting of farolitos ("little lights") at Christmastime to welcome the Christ child. Except for the age of these autos, this photo of LaFonda could have been taken one night in early December in any recent year. The farolitos consist of votive candles resting in a bed of sand in paper bags. The lights are deceptively simple to make, but give off a near-magic glow. For years, the homes and businesses of Santa Fe have competed in the use of this decoration at Christmas. Former Santa Feans have exported the idea to their new locales—sometimes to the chagrin of firefighting officials who have to be convinced that farolitos are safe! Another Yuletide custom is the use of luminarias ("piles of burning logs"), also to welcome the Christ child.

Photo by T. Harmon Parkhurst; courtesy of the Museum of New Mexico (negative no. 54312)

St. Catherine Boys

Self-sufficiency was the key to the day-to-day operation of St. Catherine Indian School in the 1930s. These young men from several locations in the Southwest baked bread as one of their many duties at the coed boarding school. Even today, students at the school do all custodial work under the supervision of the same order that has run that school since 1894, the Sisters of the Blessed Sacrament.

Photo courtesy of St. Catherine Indian School

159

Gans Store

Julius Gans was one of the first merchants to purvey Indian and Spanish crafts not only to visitors to Santa Fe, but to markets outside the Southwest. From his store, first on the east side of the Plaza and later in the Gans Building where today one finds Kahn's Shoe Store on San Francisco Street on the Plaza's south side, Gans employed "half of Chimayó and Truchas," according to his daughter Marjorie. Hundreds of people in those two villages, in many pueblos, and on the Navajo reservation weaved, potted, and created jewelry for sale at the Gans store, Southwest Arts and Crafts.

On the second floor, Ollie McKenzie, shown in the foreground here, supervised women sewing clothes made from woven cloth from such places as Chimayó. Downstairs, in the back of the retail area, many silversmiths made jewelry for sale in the front of the store. The business was begun circa 1912 on the Plaza's east side and then expanded to the corner location, across from LaFonda. McKenzie began with the firm in 1931 and worked there until 1964. She began making jackets out

of the Chimayó blankets soon after she arrived, and by the time this picture was taken she was the supervisor of forty other women who made such jackets that were exported all over the country. When World War II began, the firm had about

200 Indian blankets with an innocent traditional symbol on them: a swastika. It was decided that it had to go, so all 200 blankets had the suddenly offensive symbol cut out.

Photo courtesy of Ollie McKenzie

Hockenhull

One of a series of posed inaugural photos, this one captured the outgoing administration of Governor and Mrs. A. W. Hockenhull and the incoming one of Governor and Mrs. Clyde Tingley in 1935. Tingley served two two-year terms.

This photo was made in the Museum of Fine Arts in Santa Fe at a reception and ball for the incoming administration.

Photo by T. Harmon Parkhurst; courtesy of the Museum of New Mexico (negative no. 23087)

160

Old Post Office

Old-timers still refer to this building as "the old post office," even though it has been the home to other federal offices for more than two decades. The present main post office was constructed on its site, beside the stone-faced Federal Courthouse, against the wishes of many who wanted to preserve the Federal Oval to the west of the court building.

Photo courtesy of the Museum of New Mexico (negative no. 56431)

Santa Fe Artists

A collection of Santa Fe artists posed for this gallery photo circa 1933. From left to right: Carlos Vierra, Datus Myers, Sheldon Parsons, Theodore Van Soelen, Gerald Cassidy, and Will Shuster.

Photo courtesy of the Museum of New Mexico (negative no. 20787)

Rush

The Library Reaches People *was the title of the murals painted for the Santa Fe Public Library by Olive Rush. The murals today lead the way from the main floor to the children's section downstairs. Rush first visited Santa Fe in 1914. Six years later she purchased a house at 630 Canyon Road that had been owned by the Sena and Rodriguez families for several generations. A Quaker, Rush gave her house to the local Society of Friends. It is the society's meeting house today.*

Photo by T. Harmon Parkhurst; courtesy of the Museum of New Mexico (negative no. 74015)

Zozobra

Zozobra, an eerie but delightful fixture at Fiesta ever since Will Shuster designed it in 1926, is shown here in a still from a 1938-39 movie, Santa Fe Area Celebrations, *by Ernest Knee. Zozobra, known also as Old Man Gloom, was about to get its annual torching. Santa Fe's downtown Kiwanis Club sponsors the burning of Zozobra each Friday night of Fiesta weekend, to open the festivities. Because of the large number of onlookers, the highly combustible figure is now viewed at Magers Field at Fort Marcy Park. For many years, it was burned downtown. (Another 1930s film about Santa Fe,* A Day in Santa Fe, *was scripted by resident Lynn Riggs, author of* Green Grow the Lilacs, *which was turned into the musical* Oklahoma *in the early 1940s.)*

Photo courtesy of the State Records Center and Archives, Historic Film Collection

Mary Cabot Wheelwright

Hosteen Klah

Mary Cabot Wheelwright (left) provided the money for the Museum of Navajo Ceremonial Art, now renamed the Wheelwright Museum. Of the wealthy Cabot family of Massachusetts, she moved to the Southwest in 1918 and lived in an old house north of Santa Fe, Los Luceros, in Alcalde. She befriended a Navajo medicine man, Hosteen Klah (right), on a visit to Arizona in 1926; the museum became a reality shared by the two of them in 1937. The design was by the Santa Fe artist-architect William Penhallow Henderson; it is based on a Navajo ceremonial hogan and includes an interlocking whirling log ceiling. The building has been blessed a number of times by Navajo medicine men since its opening in "blessingway ceremonies." Today, the exhibits include more than Navajo art; they encompass many different tribes. Downstairs, a mock trading post sells Indian-made art.

Wheelwright photo by Laura Gilpin, courtesy of the Wheelwright Museum and the Amon Carter Museum; © copyright 1982, Amon Carter Museum, Fort Worth; used by permission; Klah photo courtesy of the Wheelwright Museum

Chapter Eight
1940-1960:

Atoms & Adobe

So much came and went in Santa Fe in this twenty-year period: St. Vincent Hospital was built again; Cristo Rey Church was constructed as the home for the large *reredos* of the eighteenth-century *La Castrense;* the Governor's Mansion was demolished and a new one built; the 1900 state capitol was partially torn down—and what was left was covered over with territorial stucco brown; the Santa Fe Opera began; and buildings were covered over with stucco, and *vigas* appeared where they hadn't been before in a continuing effort to make Santa Fe look the way "it ought to look."

The war came to town: Many local people went to join it, and some did not come back. An internment camp for Japanese and Japanese-Americans was established in Santa Fe. And mysterious goings-on were reported to be happening at the former site of an exclusive boys' school up in the Jemez Mountains west of town, but nobody was supposed to talk about it—even though some residents knew that a lot of strangers were showing up at addresses on Palace Avenue.

And there was a continuity to all this: Fiesta went forward with its mixture of religious and secular celebrations; painters and writers continued to paint and write. And Santa Fe, after the war, attracted even more tourists than before. This time, station wagonloads of families who stayed in motels began coming to see the famous old town.

They came for all the same reasons that the other tourists had come, and, after experiencing the history of the place, the sunsets, and the character of old-new Santa Fe, they went back home—always with souvenirs, sometimes a purchase they carried in their hands, and sometimes a visual memory of a town they found to be exciting and unusual.

Again, Santa Fe had changed—and yet it hadn't.

Reredos in Cristo Rey

The giant reredos *that originally was fashioned for La Castrense on the Plaza, then moved to La Parroquia, then left in its successor, St. Francis Cathedral, found a permanent home at last when Cristo Rey Church was built in 1939 and dedicated in 1940 to commemorate the 400th anniversary of the arrival of Coronado in New Mexico. A translation of the inscription at the bottom left and right of the* reredos *says: "As a mark of devotion of the Señor Don Francisco Antonio Marín Del Valle, Governor and Captain General of this Territory and his wife, Doña María Ignacia Martínez de Ugarte, in the year of our Lord 1761."*

Photo by Tyler Dingee; courtesy of the Museum of New Mexico (negative no. 73786)

Japanese Graves

Two Japanese who died at the Santa Fe-based internment camp are buried side by side in Rosario Cemetery. Here, the tombstone of one of them, N. Sudo, stands as one of the few reminders that such a camp ever existed within the town during World War II.

The military took over an old Civilian Conservation Corps (CCC) camp on what is now West Alameda Street (approximately the site of today's Solana Shopping Center) and converted it into a camp that held up to 2,100 Japanese and Japanese-Americans at one time. Few Japanese or Americans of Japanese descent were living in the area (and those who were were not interned); most of the internees came from the West Coast. Birth and death dates on both tombstones indicate that the two campmates probably died of old age.

Photo by John Sherman

Navy Day

These young men were recruits being sworn into service on Navy Day in 1942, the first full year of World War II for the United States. The men, flanked by a large, attentive audience, stood at the edge of the Plaza in front of the Palace of the Governors. Men already in the navy were at the right.

Photo courtesy of the State Records Center and Archives, Department of Development Collection

Adobes

Some of the 180,000 adobes that were necessary to build Cristo Rey Church were laid out to dry in the sun, an ancient process that originated when the Spanish began making bricks out of adobe and straw, as contrasted to the solid "puddling" of the walls of adobe buildings by the Pueblo Indians. The church, designed by John Gaw Meem, is still believed to be the largest structure ever made of adobe.

Photo courtesy of the Museum of New Mexico (negative no. 59238)

Manhattan Project

The Manhattan Project, that hush-hush group of men and women who developed the atomic bomb at such places as nearby Los Alamos, maintained an office in the Trujillo Plaza on East Palace Avenue. A narrow entrance, with a grille, did not invite passersby to make casual visits to the offices. The men and women who were to bring about the birth of the bomb reported to the offices of this innocent-looking plaza before being whisked off to Los Alamos.

Photo courtesy of the State Records Center and Archives, Historic Santa Fe Foundation Collection

State Champs

St. Michael's High School claimed the state basketball championship in 1942. Other top teams are shown in this composite photo.

Photo courtesy of the Christian Brothers and St. Michael's High School

South Side Plaza

Few stores shown in this 1940s photo remain on the three commercial sides of the Plaza; instead, most of the businesses are geared to tourists. Much of the change from local- to tourist-oriented stores took place in the very recent past and is a matter of debate among Santa Feans.

Photo by New Mexico State Tourist Bureau; courtesy of the State Records Center and Archives

East Side Plaza

Hinkel's occupied the corner location in the Catron Block in this 1940s-era photo. The Santa Fe Railway ticket office at the right-hand corner was designed by artist-architect William Penhallow Henderson, who also designed the Wheelwright Museum. Hinkel's replaced the White House store on the corner location in the early 1940s; it was succeeded by Hubbard's in the mid-1950s. In the 1960s, Dunlap's took over the corner, then relinquished the space to the Guarantee in 1976, when it moved to the former J.C. Penney's location on the south side of the Plaza. Penney's, in turn, moved to the new DeVargas Shopping Mall. The Guarantee had been a Santa Fe store since 1922, but it had sold only shoes until the expansion into the Palace Avenue and Old Santa Fe Trail corner spot made it possible for it to have room to become a women's clothing store as well.

Photo by New Mexico State Tourist Bureau; courtesy of the State Records Center and Archives

La Conquistadora

La Conquistadora is carried by young Santa Fe women in this 1947 photo. In the background to the right is Sena Plaza; to the left is the present Federal Building, then the U.S. Post Office. La Conquistadora continues to be carried through the streets annually on Corpus Christi Day, when she is taken to Rosario Chapel for a few days and then returned to her own chapel within the walls of the cathedral. The ancient statue was the subject of much concern when she was stolen in the spring of 1973, months after the statue of the Archangel Michael was stolen from his place at the altar in San Miguel Chapel. Both were recovered from the same hiding place.

Photo by Robert Martin

Corpus Christi

A Corpus Christi procession circa 1948 passed by the Sena family altar on the Palace Avenue side of Sena Plaza. When the heirs to the property deeded it to Senator Bronson Cutting, Martha R. White, and Amelia E. White in 1927, the right to erect this altar was retained. For many years after (until the late 1960s), it was a part of the Corpus Christi celebration. In this photo, some Sisters of Loretto who taught at the Loretto Academy at that time and girls on their way to first communion, walked past Sena Plaza and the old family altar.

Photo courtesy of Amalia Sena Sanchez

Magoffin House

The Magoffin house in 1949 was the Old Santa Fe Trading Post, not an altogether inappropriate end for the home of some of Santa Fe's best-known traders. The "closing out sale" sign signaled the end for the structure itself too. It was torn down soon after. Today the site is the parking lot for LaFonda.

After the Magoffins left town, the house was occupied by a succession of other Santa Feans, including E. A. (Eugene Allen) Fiske, who purchased the house in 1881. His second wife, Josie Fiske, sold the property in 1910 after his death.

Photo by M. J. Hoban; courtesy of Museum of New Mexico (negative 30464)

Magoffin Party

The historic Magoffin house where Susan Shelby Magoffin stayed in 1846 when she and her husband arrived in Santa Fe on the heels of Brigadier-General Kearny was torn down in 1949. The night before the razing of the historic house across from St. Francis Cathedral, a party was given in the house, and guests wore historic costumes. Shown here, second from left, is Will Shuster, and to his left is Adelina Otero-Warren. She came dressed as Doña Tules and tried her hand at the gaming table during the evening.

Photo by M. J. Hoban; courtesy of the Museum of New Mexico (negative no. 30447)

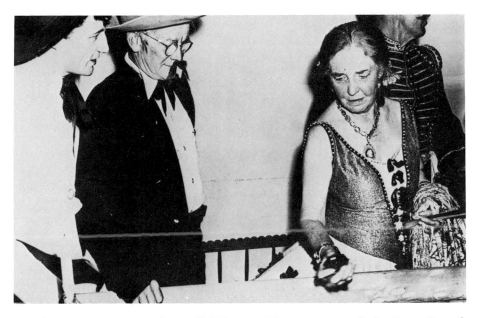

Woolworth's

Woolworth's still occupies this space on the south side of the Plaza, although the building looks a bit different today from the outside. This photo was taken before the portales were extended all around the Plaza. (The photo is from 1949, and the portales were constructed in 1967.) Goodman's later moved to a larger location further west on San Francisco Street and went out of business in 1981. The Contemporary Craftsman gallery occupies the second Goodman's location.

Photo courtesy of the State Records Center and Archives, Department of Development Collection

Points

At 212 Agua Fria, circa 1950-53, this photo was made of the Points Drive-In, a popular hangout. Souders Furniture Company was to the right.

Photo courtesy of the Museum of New Mexico (negative no. 29171)

Dome Removal

Another victim of the drive to "early up" buildings in Santa Fe, the 1900 capitol was drastically renovated and covered in territorial style brown stucco to become today's Bataan Memorial Building. Visitors to that building today can climb the stairs and see the underside of this dome and view some of the design left intact—or almost so—in the interior of this building that was being so dramatically changed in this April 1951 photo.

Photo by Harold D. Walter; courtesy of the State Records Center and Archives; Department of Development Collection

Columns

During 1950-53, the state capitol was shorn of its dome and pillars—and a lot more—and covered, for the most part, by a territorial style facade. The pillars ended up in a variety of places, including this business location on Baca Street. The Ionic pillars stand outside this office today, causing puzzlement, to be sure, for newcomers to the city.

Photo courtesy of the State Records Center and Archives, Pic Firman Collection

Loretto Chapel

The white altar of Our Lady of Light Chapel (also called Loretto Chapel to signify its connection to the now-closed Loretto Academy for Girls) is as striking today as it was when it was first installed in 1878. The interior illustrates the French influence of the chapel built on the grounds of the academy. Today the historic chapel is joined to the Inn at Loretto, which occupies the space previously taken up by the school. The chapel is administered by the Historic Santa Fe Foundation.

Photo by George Thompson; courtesy of the Museum of New Mexico (negative no. 56376)

St. Michael's Plan

This was the architect's version of what St. Michael's College (later named the College of Santa Fe) was to look like at its new Cerrillos road location. Few of these buildings were ever constructed; instead, several of the barracks left by the Bruns General Hospital are still in use by the college.

Photo by Tyler Dingee; courtesy of the State Records Center and Archives, Dale Bullock Collection

MASTER PLAN - ST. MICHAELS COLLEGE

New St. V's

The Most Reverend Edwin V. Byrne, archbishop of the Archdiocese of Santa Fe, put mortar on the cornerstone of the new St. Vincent Hospital in 1951. The hospital served Santa Fe until 1977, when the present St. Vincent's was opened on St. Michael's Drive.

Photo by Tyler Dingee; courtesy of the Museum of New Mexico (negative no. 67793)

Meem at Vincent's

A solemn-looking John Gaw Meem waited while Archbishop Byrne blessed the main kitchen area of the new St. Vincent's Hospital on January 4, 1953. Meem was the architect for the structure that overlooks St. Francis Cathedral. It was a successor to several other institutions run by the Sisters of Charity, the group of nursing sisters brought to Santa Fe by Archbishop Lamy in the nineteenth century. In 1982, five years after the present St. Vincent's opened on St. Michael's Drive, the 1954 building was renamed La Villa Rivera in honor of Father Reynaldo Rivera, a Santa Fe-born priest slain earlier that year. La Villa Rivera contains state office space and a nursing home.

Photo by Tyler Dingee; courtesy of the Museum of New Mexico (negative no. 67756)

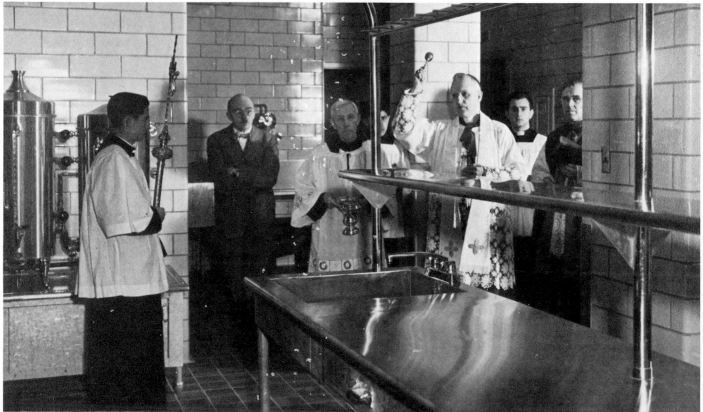

Sociedad Folklorica

The officers of the Sociedad Folklorica for 1954 were (left to right): Ramona Pert, treasurer; Lasha Casados, first vice-president; Anita Thomas, president; and Alicia Romero, second vice-president. The purposes of the Sociedad, founded in 1935, are to preserve the Spanish language, culture, and customs. The women posed in their Fiesta costumes.

Photo by Lord's Studio; courtesy of the New Mexican

Shuster and Zozobra

Will Shuster stood with the head of his "baby," Zozobra, days before one of the Fiestas found Old Man Gloom once again the object of scorn—and fire. Shuster; Dana Johnson, editor of the New Mexican, and archaeologist Sylvanus Morley came up with the idea of Zozobra for inclusion in the Fiesta celebrations of 1926. Each year Zozobra is completely rebuilt under the supervision of the Downtown Kiwanis Club.

Photo by James Coleman; courtesy of the State Records Center and Archives, Dale Bullock Collection

Chalee and Houser

Pop Chalee, of Taos Pueblo, and Allan Houser, a Fort Sill Apache, discussed the Navajo's art tradition in the Wheelwright Museum in the early 1950s. Both Chalee and Houser are very successful artists today.

Photo by Margaret McKittrick; courtesy of the Wheelwright Museum

Loretto Rear

From the rear, this was the campus of the Loretto Academy for Girls, run by the Sisters of Loretto. The chapel of Our Lady of Light, also called the Loretto Chapel, is near the left center of this photo. Today, only the chapel remains of this campus.

Photo courtesy of the State Records Center and Archives

James Stewart

Turnabout was fair play in this 1954 photo of Tesuque Pueblo Indians taking photos of film star Jimmy Stewart, on location for The Man from Laramie. It's not uncommon for Santa Fe-area people to appear as extras in films being made in northern New Mexico (sometimes right in Santa Fe).

Photo courtesy of the State Records Center and Archives, Dale Bullock Collection

A STORE BUILDING

REMODELLED FROM OLD FIRST NATIONAL BANK BUILDING, SANTA FE, N.M.

MEEM, ZEHNER, HOLIEN, & ASSOCIATES—ARCHITECTS, SANTA FE

Rendering

This architect's rendering of 1957 shows the transformation of the old First National Bank building (built 1912) on the east side of the Plaza into a Santa Fe style storefront. Today, the Kiva Trading Post occupies this building. The top floor has a solid front, rather than the windows shown here. The transformation was designed by the architectural firm headed by John Gaw Meem for Levine's Department Store, the first occupant after the departure of the bank.

Photo courtesy of the Zimmerman Library, John Gaw Meem Collection, University of New Mexico

Aerial View

This 1956 aerial view of Santa Fe highlights College Street heading out of town on the left and Don Gaspar Avenue on the right. St. Michael's College is in the lower left-hand corner of the photo and includes San Miguel as part of its campus.

Photo by Tyler Dingee; courtesy of the Museum of New Mexico (negative no. 74146)

Waltz

Waltz of the Toreadors *was the name of this Community Theatre production of 1958. In front is Wally Sargent as Gaston; and in the rear are Sharon Henshaw (left) as Estelle and Mary Kay Lourdes as Sedonia. The Jean Anouilh play was presented at the St. Michael's College Playhouse as part of the Community Theatre's 1958-59 season.*

The Community Theatre was founded in 1922; it continues to present entertaining dramatic and musical productions to Santa Fe audiences from its home on historic DeVargas Street.

Photo courtesy of the State Records Center and Archives, Dale Bullock Collection

Spiral

The famous spiral staircase in the Loretto Chapel is no longer walked upon, but around 1960 these young Loretto Academy choir singers held forth on it in the old church. The academy closed its doors in 1967, and its girl students were integrated with the boys at St. Michael's High School. When the chapel was completed in 1878, no staircase had been built to reach the choir loft. The builders had felt there was insufficient room to construct a safe one. The Sisters of Loretto prayed for aid; shortly thereafter, a carpenter appeared who built this circular staircase without the use of nails or other visible means of support. He left without waiting to be paid.

Legend says it was the work of St. Joseph, the carpenter saint. It is probable that it was the work of Johann Hadwiger, an Austrian-born carpenter who had heard about the sisters' plight while in Colorado. Though the story of the "miracle" surrounding the building of this staircase seems to have been disproved, it does not detract from the beauty of the finely carved wood or the loveliness of the rest of the stone church.

Lord's Studio photo; courtesy of the Museum of New Mexico (negative no. 14722)

St. Catherine's Aerial View

This aerial view of St. Catherine Indian School shows many buildings that are still actively used. The campus has expanded to several other buildings, as well. The front portion of the large structure on the right is the original 1887 building. Rosario Chapel is at the left center of this photo, within the cemetery of the same name, across the road from the school. The mausoleum near the school belonged to the Manderfield family. The National Cemetery continues around the perimeter of the school to the right. The large vacant space across the road from Rosario Cemetery is now the site of DeVargas Shopping Mall, which opened in 1976.

Photo by Tyler Dingee; courtesy of the Museum of New Mexico (negative no. 74125)

Governor's Mansion

The Governor's Mansion, built in 1909, went by the wayside in 1955. In 1951 the state legislature allocated money to build the present territorial style residence on Mansion Drive. Though structurally sound, the mansion was destroyed to make way for a capitol complex. That included the drastic alteration of the 1900 state capitol, seen earlier in these pages.

Mugatt photo; courtesy of the Museum of New Mexico (negative no. 56414)

Van Dresser House

The Peter Van Dresser house at 1002½ Canyon Road was described by one architectural writer as "the oldest continuously operating solar house in America." The house was built several decades ago and was later purchased by Van Dresser, who equipped it with the solar collectors shown here. Solar energy is becoming a big business in Santa Fe, and many homes and businesses are being equipped or built with passive or active solar systems, although most homes continue to depend on conventional methods for heating and cooling.

Photo by John Sherman

182

Chapter Nine
1960-1980:

Decades of Growth

Art became a bigger and bigger drawing card for Santa Fe during these two decades. Art galleries, once a rarity in twentiety-century Santa Fe, were found by the end of the 1970s all over the downtown and up and down Canyon Road.

Santa Fe had always attracted well-known people, so it was no surprise when many more of them moved into and just outside the town during this period—and nobody bothered them. Santa Feans took pride in allowing the rich and famous, as well as anyone "different," to coexist with the rest of the citizenry.

Tourism and government employment continued to be the mainstay of the local economy. A hotel replaced the Loretto Academy, and Santa Fe High School and St. Michael's High School moved out and were replaced by government offices. Local, county, state, and federal governments employed a large part of the population that was not directly involved in tourism. A new building added to the state capitol complex, the Roundhouse, opened in 1966.

The character of the downtown changed with the disappearance of the schools and the taking over of old establishments by new ones that catered more to the tourist than to the average Santa Fean. Many residents began more vigorously to promote the cause of historic preservation.

Despite all the changes going on, people were still attracted to Santa Fe's sheer beauty and the beauty of the mountains that surround it, to the variety of cultures, and to the festive occasions that are such a part of Santa Fe life.

More and more cultural groups began making Santa Fe their home, and orchestra, chorale groups, ballet, chamber music groups, and theater became part of the established scene to complement the rich cultural life that already existed. The Santa Fe Opera lost its first house to fire, but began rebuilding immediately and ended up with a wooden structure that is a showpiece in the piñon-studded hills north of the city.

By the end of the 1970s, the city had become a community of almost 50,000, with many more people living in the nearby hills. Despite a surge of growth, Santa Fe remained a friendly place, with an ambiance that did not go unnoticed. Many of the toursits came back—as residents.

Altar Screen

The altar screen of the San Miguel Chapel has been on view for almost two centuries. (Note the 1798 date at the bottom.) The Archangel Michael, for whom the church and school were named, stands at the middle bottom of the screen, just above the crucifix. This statue, second only in importance in Santa Fe to La Conquistadora, was stolen in 1972. A few months later, La Conquistadora disappeared, some said, to find San Miguel and bring him back. Despite attempts to get ransom money for the statues (and for the two circular paintings in this photograph), the culprits were apprehended, and the statues and paintings were returned to Santa Fe.

Photo by Tyler Dingee; courtesy of the Museum of New Mexico (negative no. 91819)

Nusbaum House

The Nusbaum house, home at one time or another to Governor Henry Connelly, the Spiegelberg family, and Dora and Simon Nusbaum, is shown here in July 1960, a few months before it was torn down. Attempts were made to save it, but to no avail. (Today on this site are the Greer Building and a parking lot across from the main branch of the public library on Washington Avenue.) Its destruction in 1961 led to the establishment of the Historic Santa Fe Foundation, which is dedicated to historic preservation.

Photo by Tyler Dingee; courtesy of the Museum of New Mexico (negative no. 91901)

deVargas Staff

The men accompanying Don Diego deVargas (Fernando Delgado, not shown) at the 1960 Fiesta were, left to right: Harold Valencia (portraying Don Fernado Durán y Cháves); Eduardo Montoya (Don Lázaro de Mezquia); Raymond Abeyta (Don Juan de Almazán); Patricio Lopez (Padre Salvador de San Antonio); and Gilbert G. Duran (Don Luis Granillo). The queen that year was Sylvia Carillo.

deVargas, the queen and the many members of the Fiesta contingent make several dozen appearances at community gatherings and clubs in the frenetic days preceding Fiesta each year. Always in costumes, they are accompanied on these rounds by a mariachi band; the total effect is aimed at getting the populace excited about the upcoming Fiesta weekend. Most Santa Feans need a little encouragement to get ready to enjoy the annual events.

Photo by Gilbert's Studios; courtesy of the State Records Center and Archives, Dale Bullock Collection

College, Aerial View

St. Michael's College moved from its downtown location to this site on Cerrillos Road in 1947, when the Christian Brothers purchased the former property, Bruns General Hospital, from the army. Some of these barracks remain in use today, but the campus has been graced, meantime, with more permanent struc-

tures, including a library complex; a theater; and classroom buildings of brick and stone. The school's name was later changed to the College of Santa Fe.

At the left, along Cerrillos Road, today one finds College Plaza shopping center. Bruns was built in 1942, when Santa Fe contained a little more than 20,000

inhabitants. It was named for the late Colonel Earl Harvey Bruns who had been regarded as one of the foremost authorities on pulmonary tuberculosis. The hospital closed at the end of 1946.

Photo by Tyler Dingee; courtesy of the Museum of New Mexico (negative no. 74158)

U.S. Stamp

Tyler Dingee air-brushed one of his photographs to remove telephone lines and other non-historic paraphernalia in order to provide the U.S. Post Office with a photo of the venerable Palace of the Governors for this stamp. One-half million first-day covers were issued in Santa Fe on June 17, 1960, to commemorate the 350th anniversary of the founding of the town. Eleven days of celebration (June 15-26) were devoted to the 350th. On Lew Wallace Day, Ben Hur Drive was dedicated, and Metro-Goldwyn-Mayer gave a print of the film Ben Hur, which was buried in a time capsule. Special guests at the celebration were two direct descendants of Don Diego deVargas who lived in the ancestral deVargas home in Madrid, Spain.

Photo courtesy of the U.S. Postal Service

Guadalupe Church

A new Guadalupe Church was opened in 1961 to the rear of the late eighteenth-century structure. In 1976 this older church was remodeled (the latest of several changes), and reopened for many community functions, such as art shows, musical events, and films, and to accommodate the many tourists who wished to see inside the old building and view the 1783 altar painting. In the front of this photo were the tracks for the old "Chili Line" (Denver and Rio Grande Railroad) that ran from Antonito, Colorado, to the depot just south of Guadalupe Church (where Tomasita's Restaurant is now located).

Photo courtesy of the Museum of New Mexico (negative no. 15143)

Mural Restoration

John Pogzeba directed the restoration of the Gerald Cassidy murals circa 1962 so they could be installed in the U.S. Post Office on Federal Place. The portion standing on the back wall shows Francisco Vásques de Coronado gazing at the Indians he met at Hawikuh, one of the villages of Zuni Pueblo. The Indians return the gaze from the companion mural.

Photo courtesy of the Museum of New Mexico (negative no. 42656)

St. John's

It seemed only fitting that the old city of Santa Fe be chosen as the second campus site of St. John's College, founded as King William's School in Annapolis, Maryland, in 1696 (and chartered as St. John's College in 1784). In 1964 the Santa Fe campus was established on Camino de Cruz Blanca; it draws students from many states to study the Great Books curriculum which both St. John's campuses use. "St. Johnnies," such as those pictured here, study more than 100 classic works that span many centuries and countries of origin—and also more "mundane" subjects such as chemistry lab.

Photo courtesy of St. John's College

Cerrillos Road

You can barely see the distant mountainside forest for the trees—of light poles, signs, telephone poles, and other distractions along busy Cerrillos Road. In 1964, the date of this photo, the main artery to roads leading to Albuquerque, sixty miles south, looked little different, in essence, than it does today, although many of the businesses have changed, and fast-food restaurants have replaced many of the hometown variety. Further downtown, in the Historic Zone, strict control is placed on signboards, and each addition to a building is carefully studied—and approved or disapproved.

Photo courtesy of the Museum of New Mexico (negative no. 29830)

187

Stake Driving

A group of former governors of New Mexico attended the stake-driving ceremony for the new state capitol on June 18, 1964. Two years later, the building opened. Shown here, left to right, in the front row, were former governors Richard C. Dillon (1927-30); A. W. Hockenhull (1933-34); John E. Miles (1939-42); John F. Simms, Jr. (1955-56); John Burroughs (1959-60); Tom Bolack (1962).

Photo by Milo Crawford; courtesy of the Museum of New Mexico (negative no. 10396)

Greer Garson

Actress Greer Garson (on the left in the white coat) attended the dedication of the Fogelson Library Center on the College of Santa Fe campus in 1970. She had previously built the school's Greer Garson Theatre, which opened in 1966. Her husband, E. E. "Buddy" Fogelson, had likewise funded the library. The couple maintain the Forked Lightning Ranch outside nearby Pecos.

Photo courtesy of the College of Santa Fe

Roundhouse

This fisheye lens distorts the inside of the 1966 executive-legislative building, the Roundhouse, but it helps reveal why the building has such a nickname. Built purportedly to resemble a traditional Pueblo Indian kiva, the building is one of the most unusual state office buildings in the country. The Zia Pueblo sun sign, used on the state flag, is seen here in the floor of the central lobby. At the top is a large skylight which lets some of the famous New Mexico sun into the building.

Photo by Robert Martin; courtesy of the Museum of New Mexico (negative no. 68301)

Roundhouse Aerial View

New Mexico got its fifth capitol building when the Roundhouse was opened in 1966, one year before this aerial shot was taken. Although most Santa Feans refer to this building as the capitol, it is actually an executive-legislative building that is part of the whole capitol complex (that includes the Bataan Building and Mabry Hall, directly behind the Roundhouse in this photo). The first capitol was the Palace of the Governors built in 1610; the second was constructed in 1886 and burned six years later; the third was built in 1900, and then covered under the fourth one, now referred to by many residents as "the old capitol" (the Bataan Building). The building nearest the Roundhouse is the state library; beyond that is the state supreme court.

Photo by Dick Kent; courtesy of the Museum of New Mexico (negative no. 91176)

189

Opera Fire

Still the chief cultural attraction of Santa Fe for many visitors and residents alike, the Santa Fe Opera got its start in 1957 under the management of John Crosby. The driving force behind the world-renowned opera had been a student at the Los Alamos Ranch School (later the site of the Los Alamos Scientific Laboratories and the top-secret Manhattan Project during World War II). His love of the area drew him back to Santa Fe to found the opera. Disaster struck, however, in 1967, when a fire destroyed the opera house; out of this misfortune came today's dramatic and beautiful wooden theater in the hills north of the city.

Photo courtesy of the Santa Fe Opera

Opera Roof

Today's Santa Fe Opera performances are enjoyed in this stunning building. To the left, the rounded roof covers the stage, orchestra, and some of the audience, while the one to the right protects the balcony and some of the main floor. During July and August each summer, many American and world premieres of new and recently-discovered works are performed, as well as old favorites. An ambitious apprentice program allows audiences to hear promising new voices—and gives apprentices a chance to perform to appreciative full houses.

Photo by Robert L. Carpenter; courtesy of the Museum of New Mexico (negative no. 53270)

Loretto Chapel

After the fire that destroyed the old Loretto Academy convent in 1973, and before the construction of the present Inn at Loretto on that site, this photo was made of the Loretto Chapel. LaFonda is visible in the background on the right. The photographer was standing on the present site of the inn. During the razing of the convent, a fire started. Anxious Santa Feans watched the fire almost take the chapel that had been one of the French artisans' contributions to Santa Fe.

Photo courtesy of the State Records Center and Archives, Historic Santa Fe Foundation Collection

School of American Research

Amelia White donated her home and surrounding acreage to the School of American Research for its headquarters on Garcia Street. Miss White also donated a small park to the city; it is named after her.

Photo by David Noble; courtesy of the School of American Research

IAIA Faculty

The Institute of American Indian Arts was founded in 1962 as an arts school for American Indian youth from across the country. It was located for many years on Cerrillos Road (where the Santa Fe Indian School is now), and where its museum is still to be found, but classes for the institute now meet on the College of Santa Fe campus. Here, the 1973 faculty got together for this group picture by one of their own, Kay Wiest. Wiest came from New York in 1946 to paint Indians. "Instead," she said, "I sent the Indians (paintings) back, and stayed myself."

Seated, front, left to right, Terrence W. Schubert, jewelry; Josephine Wapp, traditional techniques. Standing, first row, left to right: Seymour Tubis, etching; Otellie Loloma, ceramics and ceramic sculpture; Rolland R. Meinholtz, drama, theater; Lloyd Kiva New, director, silkscreen; Kay Wiest, painting, commercial art, photography; T. D. Allen, writing; Allan Houser, sculpture; Fritz Scholder, contemporary painting; Michael McCormick, metal sculpture. Back row, left to right: Neil Parsons, contemporary painting; Ralph A. Pardington, ceramics; Leo Bushman, painting; Jim McGrath, assistant art director; and Louis Ballard, music.

Photo by Kay Wiest

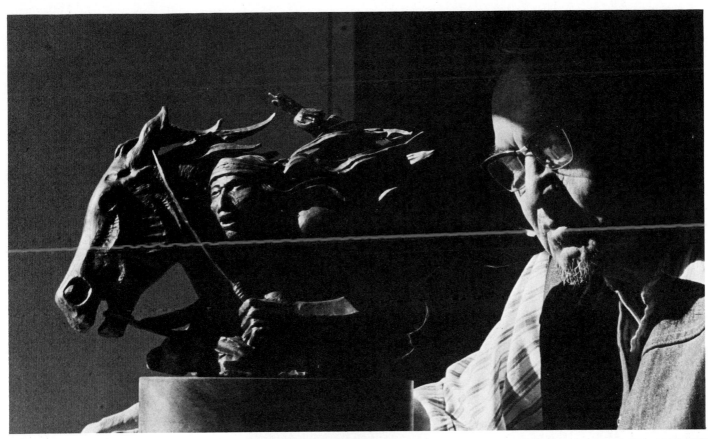

Houser Sculpture

Sculptor Allan Houser's face seems reflected in his bronze sculpture. Houser, a Fort Sill Apache, has lived and worked in Santa Fe for many years. His work, like that of many Indians of the Southwest, is for sale in a city well known for its galleries and shops selling Indian made arts and crafts.

Photo by Kay Wiest

Laura Gilpin

Famed photographer Laura Gilpin made Santa Fe her home, as did (and do) so many other well-known artists, writers, and photographers. She is shown here visiting with students at the Institute of American Indian Arts circa 1973-74.

Gilpin began photographing around 1910. One of her most famous collections of photographs is The Enduring Navajo, first published in 1968.

Photo by Kay Wiest

Plaza Renovation

The ancient San Francisco Street received one more facelift in 1973-74 when the Plaza was being renovated. The renovation had begun in 1966-67 when the portales shown here were installed all the way around the Plaza.

Photo by David Margolis; courtesy of the Museum of New Mexico (negative no. 90300)

Opera Performers

Some people come to Santa Fe for things of great beauty; others come for the arts. Those who go to the Santa Fe Opera have the chance to experience both. In this 1974 production of Lulu by Alban Berg, the audience saw and heard William Parker as the Acrobat (left), Claudia Catania as the Student, and Andrew Foldi as Schigolch.

Photo by Cradoc Bagshaw; courtesy of the Santa Fe Opera

House Mural

This mural, on a building at 529 West San Francisco Street (now a law firm), is typical of several such murals painted in Santa Fe in the 1970s. This one was painted by Jerry Garduño, Sam Leyba, and Albert Leyba in 1973-75 as part of the Los Artes Guadalupaños de Aztlan muralist movement.

Photo by John P. Conron; courtesy of the city of Santa Fe and the photographer

La Conquistadora Chapel

Tucked on the north side of St. Francis Cathedral (the only portion of the eighteenth-century La Parroquia that survives) is the small chapel of La Conquistadora. This small statue has served as the symbol of Hispanic unity in Santa Fe since she was first brought here in 1625.

Photo by Robert Brewer: courtesy of the Museum of New Mexico (negative no. 65144)

195

Rodeo

The horse and rider were about to go their separate ways when this photo was taken at the Rodeo de Santa Fe. Each summer, the rodeo grounds on the south side of the city are home to bucking broncos, lassoing cowboys, and all the other elements of a full-scale show. The rodeo began in 1949. El Toro, a papier-mâché bull that is the symbol of the Rodeo de Santa Fe, was created and built by Will Shuster a few years later. Shuster also created the Fiesta's Zozobra.

Photo courtesy of the New Mexican

Alexander Girard

Alexander Girard (right) adjusted a piece of a large doll house being readied for an exhibition (left) at the Museum of International Folk Art, a unit of the Museum of New Mexico. The museum is located on Camino Lejo between the Wheelwright Museum and the Labora- *tory of Anthropology on Santa Fe's southeast side. Girard and his wife Susan have donated an enormously large collection of folk art to the museum (106,000 pieces in 1978—a donation that increased the museum's collections fivefold). The wing named after them,* *which contains much of that collection amassed from travels around the world, opened in 1982. The whimsical pieces of art delight the children in all of us.*

Photo courtesy of the Museum of International Folk Art

Chapter Ten
1980-:

The Discovery of Santa Fe

By the 1980s, Santa Fe had long been established as a place to go, if not to live.

And, continuing a tradition begun decades before, well-known people, especially those in the arts, purchased homes on a *camino* or *calle* of Santa Fe to spend part or all of the year here in view of the sunsets and the mountains—the Jemez, the Ortiz, and the Sangre de Cristo.

Also in the 1980s, Santa Fe was discovered by the national media. That controversy continues to entertain and enrage Santa Feans. The city was dubbed "in" by some magazines and newspapers after their reporters and photographers descended upon the old capital. They shared their experiences with the rest of the country, but it was disputed whether they had shared the Santa Feans' as well. Most of the media virtually ignored the Indian and Spanish elements of Santa Fe and presented only a portion of the people of this city, thereby missing the richness and vibrancy of a tri-cultural community.

It is that very mixture of cultures, with each retaining certain features to itself, that gives such a distinctive character to the old Villa de Santa Fe.

Archbishop Sanchez

The Reverend Roberto Sanchez, Archbishop of the Archdiocese of Santa Fe, blessed the Fiesta Queen of 1980, Elizabeth Roybal, during the religious ceremonies in St. Francis Cathedral associated with the annual Fiesta. Though Fiesta contains a lot of frivolity, there is, as with all such celebrations, a deep religious base.

Photo by Barbaraellen Koch, courtesy of the New Mexican

Art Gallery

By the 1980s there were at least 100 art galleries in Santa Fe, such as the Elaine Horwitch Gallery (shown here), that were selling an enormous variety of works of art. Some galleries specialized in Southwestern art; others were even more specific and dealt only in Native American work, but sculpture and painting of many parts of the world and created by many different generations were for sale in galleries throughout the city.

Most galleries were located downtown, in the Plaza area, or were on or near Canyon Road, a street associated in the twentieth century with art and artists. Santa Fe had become by 1980 the third largest art market in the United States, surpassed only by New York and Chicago, respectively. Because of its longtime reputation as an art center, it continued to attract artists from all over the country—and buyers from around the nation as well. Despite the business and money the art galleries brought into Santa Fe, many Santa Feans were disturbed by the disappearance of old-time, local stores from the downtown area.

Photo courtesy of the Elaine Horwitch Gallery

Prison-reform Demonstrator

Santa Fe received worldwide attention in early 1980 when a bloody prison riot resulted in incredible destruction to the state prison south of the city and the loss of thirty-three lives. Here, a demonstrator shared her concern at one of the many gatherings after the riot where prison reform was on the minds—and tongues—of many Santa Feans.

Photo by Barbaraellen Koch; courtesy of the New Mexican

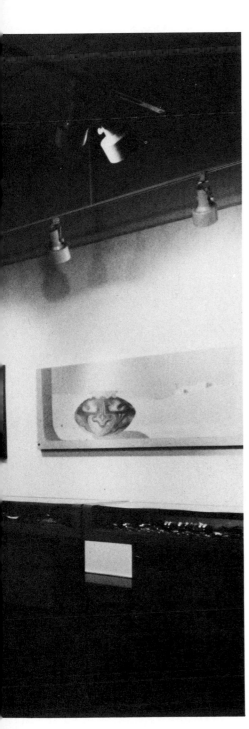

Festival Theatre

Michael York portrayed Cyrano de Bergerac in the play of the same name at the brand-new Santa Fe Festival Theatre in summer 1980. This theater, operating out of the Armory for the Arts (a former armory that is now a theater) on Old Pecos Trail, was one of several arts groups presenting professional-level work to the Santa Fe community and the large number of visitors interested in the dramatic and musical scene of a very culture-minded town.

Photo courtesy of the Santa Fe Festival Theatre

Majorie Tallchief

The Osage Indian ballerina Majorie Tallchief carefully watched the movements of a young Santa Fe danseuse when she was the guest artist at a 1981 summer workshop at the Greer Garson Theatre at the College of Santa Fe. Her sister, Maria Tallchief, is another well-known ballerina.

Photo by Barbaraellen Koch; courtesy of the New Mexican

202

Mural Dedication

. Zara Kriegstein spoke to the crowd assembled to witness the unveiling of the large mural on the Guadalupe Street side of the State Records Center and Archives in September 1980. Kriegstein was one of the muralists; others in the photo who worked on the project include Frederico Vigil, right; Rose Mary Stearns and Cassandra Harris, right and left, respectively, behind the woman in the white blouse (who was not a part of the dedication, but who had come up on stage to make a protest). Part of the cloth that had covered the mural prior to its dedication is shown on the right. Others also worked on the mural, but were not on stage at the dedication.

Photo by Juan Rios; courtesy of the New Mexican

Orchestra

William Kirschke conducted the Orchestra of Santa Fe in a performance at Sweeney Center. The orchestra, founded in 1974, made its debut the next year; it is one of many groups in the city that offers Santa Feans a variety of musical experiences.

Photo by Marilyn Foss; courtesy of the Orchestra of Santa Fe

Santa Fe Downs

The Santa Fe Downs on the road to Albuquerque is yet another summertime attraction of Santa Fe. Betting is legal— and as brisk as the horses. Thoroughbred and quarter horse racing takes place May through Labor Day. The downs opened in 1971.

Photo courtesy of the Santa Fe Downs

Ski Basin

The Santa Fe ski season, roughly from Thanksgiving to near Easter, draws people from many states to the slopes in the Sangre de Cristo mountains north-northwest of the city. The skiing only adds to the charm of the small city in the wintertime, when snow trims the brown adobe walls—as it has for centuries.

Photo courtesy of the New Mexican

Maria Benitez

Flamenco dancer Maria Benitez grimaced as she performed with Rafael Torres (left) and Joaquin Ruiz (right). Benitez has danced flamenco for avid Santa Fe summer audiences for several years at different hotels and clubs. She studied flamenco in Spain, and then brought it with a passion to the former Spanish colonial city of Santa Fe. Her concentration and intensity—and her lavish costumes—are trademarks of her performance.

Photo by Richard Bender; courtesy of Maria Benitez

Aerial View

Santa Fe in November 1981 had a few buildings and places in common with the Santa Fe of Urrutia when he drew his map in 1766-68. The Palace of the Governors was, of course, still on the north side of the Plaza, and San Miguel Chapel remained on what had become Old Santa Fe Trail after some changes over the centuries. The Santa Fe River, never a raging torrent, had, years before this photo was taken, become little more than a trickle because of the damming of the waters further upstream for the reservoir that serves the city.

Post-Urrutia additions (virtually everything else in the photo) include the round building in the right-center, the present Roundhouse. (North a short distance is the Plaza and the Palace.) The U.S. Courthouse and the U.S. Post Office share the Federal Oval a few blocks north of the Plaza. To the right of the oval a short distance is the empty space (the mounds are still there) where the earthen-walled Fort Marcy once was. The DeVargas Shopping Mall is the large building surrounded by a parking lot in the upper left corner. Across the street from the shopping center is Rosario Cemetery and St. Catherine Indian School.

Photo courtesy of the city of Santa Fe and Bohannan-Huston, Inc.

Chamber Music Festival

*Alicia Schachter at the piano and Ani
Kavafian at violin entertained an
audience in the eighteenth-century
Santuario de Guadalupe. They performed beneath the large canvas painting
done in Mexico in 1783. The Santa Fe
Chamber Music Festival (of which this
performance was a part) was founded by
Schachter and her husband Sheldon Rich
in 1973. The festival members have
performed not only in Santa Fe, but have
presented a series of concerts elsewhere,
including New York City.*

Lillian Gish

When film star Lillian Gish saw this photo of herself at a Santa Fe Film Festival party in 1982, she exclaimed, "This is how I feel about Santa Fe!" Gish was in town, along with Gene Kelly, Ray Bolger, Adolph Green, and Betty Comden, and many others of the film world, to help Santa Feans celebrate the theme of that year's festival, Music and the Movies. The festival, brainchild of Bill Pence, began as an annual summer celebration in 1980.

Photo by Lisa Law

Indian Woman and Child

Overleaf: There is one thing in Santa Fe older than the Palace of the Governors: the association of the Pueblo Indians with the area that is now the state capital of New Mexico. Ancient settlements and pueblos of these Native Americans were found up and down the rivers and tributaries of northern New Mexico. Descendants of those "ancient ones," or Anasazi, today may wear digital watches, but the bond between mother and child is still as strong and as loving as it was when the Spanish first came to this area in 1610 and founded a city that so many have come to love: Santa Fe.

Photo by Barbaraellen Koch; courtesy of the New Mexican

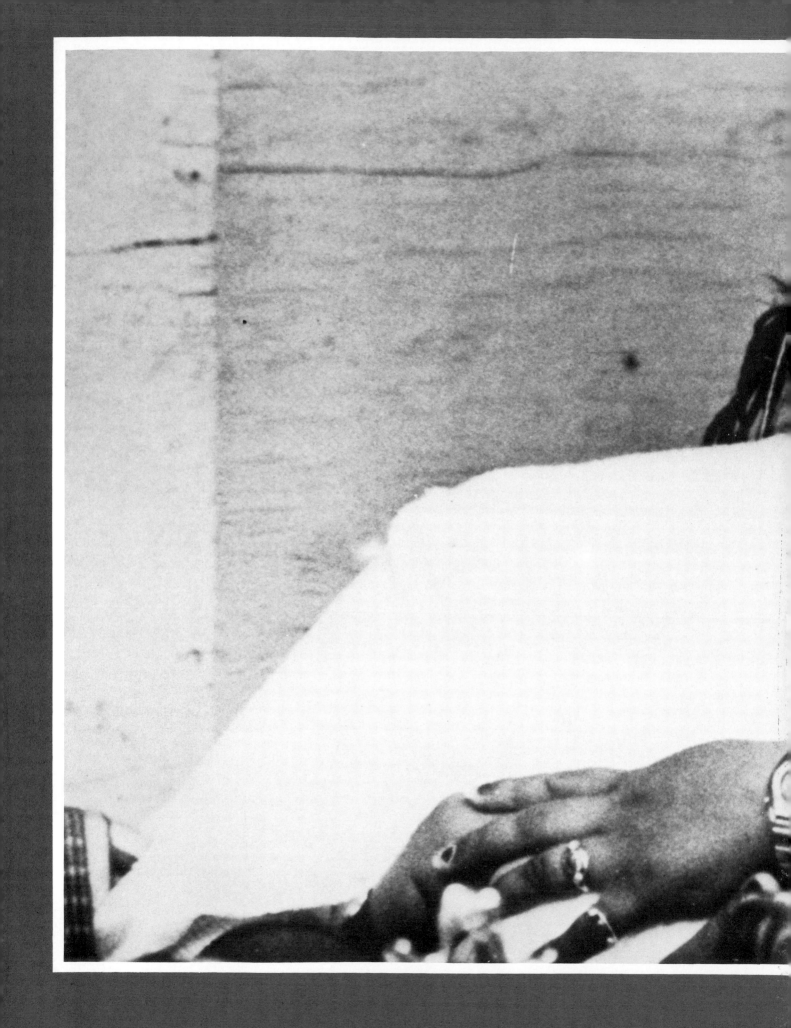

Bibliography

Chavez, Angelico. *La Conquistadora: The Auto-biography of an Ancient Statue.* Paterson, N.J.: St. Anthony Guild Press, 1954.

_____ . *Origins of New Mexico Families in the Spanish Colonial Period in Two Parts: The Seventeenth (1598-1693) and Eighteenth (1693-1821) Centuries.* Santa Fe: Historical Society of New Mexico, 1954.

Coldwell, Bro. Tim. *A History of Bruns General Hospital and its Subsequent Acquisition by St. Michael's College 1942-1947.* B. A. Research Paper, College of Santa Fe, 1977.

Dickson, D. Bruce. *Arroyo Hondo, New Mexico, Site Survey.* Santa Fe: School of American Research Press, 1979.

Drumm, Stella, Ed. *Down the Santa Fe Trail and into Mexico: Diary of Susan Shelby Magoffin 1846-1847.* New Haven: Yale University Press, 1926.

Historic Santa Fe Foundation. *Old Santa Fe Today,* 3rd edition. Albuquerque: University of New Mexico Press, 1982.

Horgan, Paul. *Lamy of Santa Fe.* New York: Farrar, Straus and Giroux, 1975.

Jenkins, Dr. Myra Ellen and Schroeder, Albert H. *Brief History of New Mexico.* Albuquerque: University of New Mexico Press, 1974.

Kelly, Daniel T. with Chauvenet, Beatrice. *The Buffalo Head.* Santa Fe: Vergara Publishing Company, 1972.

Kimball, Clark, and Smith, Marcus, M.D. *The Hospital at the End of the Santa Fe Trail.* Santa Fe: Rydal Press, 1977.

LaFarge, Oliver. *Santa Fe: The Autobiography of a Southwestern Town.* Norman: The University of Oklahoma Press, 1959.

Nusbaum, Rosemary. *The City Different and the Palace.* Santa Fe: Sunstone Press, 1978.

Pearce, T. M., ed. *Literary America 1903-1934: The Mary Austin Letters.* Westport, Conn.: Greenwood Press, 1979.

Rudisill, Richard. *Photographers of the New Mexico Territory: 1854-1912.* Santa Fe: Museum of New Mexico, 1973.

St. Michael's High School. *A Hundred Years of Service.* Santa Fe: St. Michael's College Press, 1959.

Simmons, Marc. *New Mexico: A History.* New York: W. W. Norton Company, 1977.

Stubbs, Stanley A. and Stallings, W. S., Jr. *The Excavation of Pindi Pueblo, New Mexico.* Santa Fe: Monograph no. 18 of the School of American Research, 1953.

Photo of John Sherman, author.

Photo by Jane Bakewell, **Santa Fe Reporter**

Index